DANCES OF THE TEWA
PUEBLO INDIANS

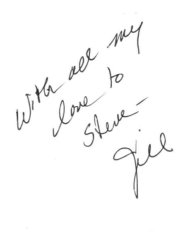

With all my love to Steve —
Jill

DANCES OF THE TEWA
PUEBLO INDIANS

EXPRESSIONS OF NEW LIFE
SECOND EDITION

JILL D. SWEET

School of American Research Press

Santa Fe, New Mexico

School of American Research
Post Office Box 2188
Santa Fe, New Mexico 87504-2188

Director: James F. Brooks
Executive Editor: Catherine Cocks
Copy Editors: Catherine Cocks and Jane Kepp
Design and Production: Cynthia Dyer
Indexer: Ina Gravitz
Proofreader: Kate Talbot
Printer: Sung In Printing

Library of Congress Cataloging-in-Publication Data

Sweet, Jill D. (Jill Drayson)
  Dances of the Tewa Pueblo Indians : expressions of new life / Jill D. Sweet.
      p. cm.
  "A School of American Research resident scholar book."
  Includes bibliographical references and index.
  ISBN 1-930618-29-8 (pbk. : alk. paper)
  1. Tewa dance. 2. Tewa Indians—Rites and ceremonies. I. Title.
E99.T35 S93 2004
793.3'1'08997494—dc22
                              2003023696

Cover: *Corn Dance* by Nora Naranjo-Morse, monotype print. Photograph by Gregory S. Morse. Frontispiece: *Route 66* © 2002 by Mateo Romero, oil and acrylic on panel and aluminum, 40 x 60

Dedicated to Andrew Garcia
and to the memories of
Antonio Garcia, Cipriano Garcia,
and Peter Garcia.

CONTENTS

ILLUSTRATION LIST

FOREWORD

The first edition of *Dances of the Tewa Pueblo Indians* served as an important presentation and explication of the ritual dances and ceremonies of the Pueblo Indians of New Mexico. In the preface to this second edition, author Jill D. Sweet argues that the research and information originally published in 1985 continue to be viable and correct today. She acknowledges, however, that her relationship with friends and informants within Native American communities has changed. This change and the acknowledgement of it are the most significant revisions the new edition offers.

Sweet consciously attempts to move herself from the front of the book as the outside expert to an interstitial place among the group of informants and friends with whom she worked. She has also tried to move the Native Americans from their supporting role as informants to a central position in the book.

Sweet has attempted this shift in emphasis in all honesty and with great integrity. She sought to identify all of the individuals pictured in the photographs used in the first edition. She tried to get her informants' permission to name them individually in the volume, and she has acknowledged her role as an outsider in the culture and societies of the Tewa Pueblo Indians. This difficult task could have easily resulted in a completely new book but instead enriches its original appeal.

I emphasize here for a moment the shifting relationship between the outside researcher and the inside, the people being researched. The winds of the post-modern world have swept over anthropology and art history during the past

Figure 1. Feast Day Thoughts © *by Nora Naranjo-Morse, monotype print; photograph by Gregory S. Morse.*

twenty-five to thirty years. New ideas and new concepts of relations have profoundly changed theoretical programs of interpretation. Only recently have these changes begun to reshape the institutions and organizations that manage the practical aspects of anthropological research around the world.

The School of American Research is a good example of an organization that seeks now to address these important changes. This second edition of *Dances of the Tewa Pueblo Indians* is one significant example of the new direction SAR is taking today. Structural changes in the connection between SAR and the Native American community and the relationship of SAR programs to each other represent a new vision of the anthropological endeavor. Like the new edition of a classic book that you hold in your hands, this vision draws deeply on a rich heritage.

Richard M. Leventhal
President
School of American Research

PREFACE
TO THE SECOND EDITION

In 1973, I began fieldwork among the Pueblo Indian villages of New Mexico, and in 1985, the School of American Research (SAR) Press published the first edition of a book based on that research. Twenty-nine years after I began the research and seventeen years after the book came out, SAR invited me to produce a revised edition. When I reread the book, however, I found that surprisingly little of it had become dated with regard to the dances, despite tremendous changes among the Pueblos in other respects. I also realized that the sort of fieldwork I had done in the 1970s would be impossible today because of dramatic changes in the academy, as well as in me and in Native American autonomy. Following this new preface, then, I present the 1985 edition in its entirety, along with a new epilogue featuring the words and images of individual Tewa people as they reflect on Pueblo dance in the twenty-first century.

Anthropology and dance ethnography, the two academic disciplines that most directly informed the original text, have gone through some interesting changes since the 1970s and 1980s. Practitioners of these related areas of inquiry have become increasingly self-conscious about taking the role of academic expert representing the "other." Perhaps this self-consciousness is the result of changing political landscapes. Anthropology and dance ethnology first developed within the context of late nineteenth-century colonialism. In contemporary post-colonial regimes, anthropologists no longer consider subjects to be culturally isolated, bounded, or insulated from worldwide shifts in political economy. The waning power of nation-states in the face of globalization has contemporary ethnographers questioning some of their most basic assumptions about the ethnographic process. Of particular concern is the issue of description, commonly referred to as a "crisis of representation." Issues of objectivity, truth, and interpretation compel researchers to ask whose story it is and who has the right to tell that story. What are the political and ethical ramifications of the ethnographer's representations for those being depicted? Can there be more than one true representation in the description of another culture? Are there ways to present both the researcher's voice and the voices of the ethnographic subjects?

These questions point to the relationship between researchers and the subjects of their research. The once academically accepted practice of the educated and well-funded scholar lording over the Indian "informant" is now suspect. Increasingly, Indians have a voice in what researchers may and may not investigate. Native people are demanding that researchers abide by their rules about what is and what is not acceptable research. Native people want researchers to produce work that can benefit their communities, and they want veto power over research that they consider frivolous or even detrimental to their people. For better or for worse, ethnographic research has forever changed as a result. These changes inspired me to reflect on my fieldwork and the writing process. They also motivated me to bring forward the voices of Native people. My hope is that this new edition will result in a more balanced, multidimensional representation of both inside and outside views of Tewa dance.

When I said that I could not conduct fieldwork today in the way I did in the 1970s, I was referring to the importance of gaining permission to launch such a study. Back then, both my dissertation adviser and a key Native consultant urged me *not* to ask formally for permission from the various tribal councils before proceeding with my project. Instead, they urged me simply to go to the dances and to watch and listen respectfully. They warned me that a formal request would only "stir things up" with the councils. I respected both of these men. My dissertation adviser was Alfonso Ortiz, a Tewa Indian from San Juan Pueblo who earned a Ph.D. from the University of Chicago and became an accomplished anthropologist. Ortiz had written a stunning ethnography titled *The Tewa World: Space, Time, Being and Becoming in a Pueblo Society* (Ortiz 1969). My central Native consultant was Tony Garcia, who had served as governor of San Juan Pueblo and had written a paper on Tewa dance preparations for the journal *Ethnomusicology* (Garcia and Garcia 1968). He had also co-authored a book on Tewa dance with the pioneer dance ethnologist Gertrude Kurath (Kurath and Garcia 1970). Nevertheless, today conducting research without explicit tribal approval would be unacceptable. Researchers must obtain permission from tribal political bodies, which must approve each project. Without such formal permission, researchers, their home institutions, and funding agencies could face professional censorship and even litigation in the courts.

In addition to these changes in the fields of anthropology and dance ethnography, personal changes in my life and career affected the way I approached this new edition. When I began writing the original book, I was a resident scholar at the School of American Research, supported by the Weatherhead Foundation, and a graduate student completing the requirements for the Ph.D. in anthropology at the University of New Mexico. I also had just received a troubling diagnosis of multiple sclerosis. What a shock! How could it be? I had, after all, been a dancer and a choreographer. But at that point, the effects of the illness did not show and I could pass as healthy. Because I was ambitious, driven by the desire for a successful career as a sociocultural anthropologist with an expertise in dance, I kept my MS diagnosis a secret and continued an active life of fieldwork, research, and, later, teaching.

When I began writing this new edition in the summer of 2002, I did so as, once again, a resident scholar at SAR, this time as an Ethel-Jane Westfeldt Bunting Fellow. But by this time, the illness had progressed and I was using a wheelchair. SAR housed me in the Wagner House on its beautiful campus because the building had been renovated recently to make it wheelchair accessible. Raymond Sweeney, who is now director of Plant Operations and Maintenance and who remembered me from my first stay at the school in 1981, kindly built a ramp for me to use in getting into my office. Nevertheless, the act of fieldwork had become tremendously challenging, and I began to have trouble going out to the dances. The year before, I had gone to see dances in a pueblo church but could not enter because of a thick adobe step. Four strong Pueblo men had come to my rescue, lifting me and my chair over the barrier. Facing such challenges has led me to refocus my goals and ambitions. Now my central concern is helping my students and readers get beyond simplistic stereotypes of Indians and see them instead as living people, many of whom are dancing in the twenty-first century. In an ironic sense, I continue to study and teach about Tewa Pueblo movement while my own mobility becomes increasingly limited.

During my twenty-two years of teaching at Skidmore College in upstate New York, I have been able to return to the pueblos once or twice a year between semesters or during sabbatical leaves. I have also brought several friends from the reservations to the college for classroom visits, seminars, and public lectures. In teaching undergraduates about Native cultures, I seek to have them experience Indians in the twenty-first century as real, living people who participate in contemporary American society. I have introduced them to Native American educators, lawyers, poets, artists, social workers, storytellers, students, and athletes. These meetings strengthen my students' understandings of both their shared humanity with Native Americans and their cultural and historical differences. They begin to see the creative ways in which contemporary Indians successfully live and work within a nation-state that continually contests their sovereignty.

In recent years, my interests have turned toward "applied anthropology" projects that could directly serve Native American communities in their struggles for self-determination. In 1994, supported by a grant from the Nonprofit Sector Research Fund of the Aspen Institute, I conducted an ethnographic evaluation of Futures for Children, an organization headquartered in Albuquerque, New Mexico. This nonprofit institution works to inspire principles of self-help within reservation communities. At the time of my study, about 60 percent of the organization's employees were Indian, but non-Indians held most of the managerial positions. This imbalance caused internal stress. After interviewing clients in Pueblo and Navajo communities where Futures had worked, I found that the organization had not always realized its ultimate goal of establishing the principle of self-help. In many cases, years of paternalism by the United States government and charity organizations competed with Futures' efforts. I also discovered that philosophical differences about Futures' efforts to keep children in school divided the organization. At the heart of the debate was the requirement that sponsors send money directly to the students. Some regarded the small donation, typically $150 annually for school supplies, as charity, in violation of the organization's efforts to emphasize self-help.

After reading these findings, Futures for Children requested that my assessment remain unpublished and available only internally, but it did implement some of the changes I suggested. The organization also agreed to a co-authored and jointly presented paper for the 1995 annual meeting of the Society for Applied Anthropology (Sweet and Bennett 1995). The paper represented a true collaboration between me and Ruby Bennett, who at the time was the only Native program director in the Futures organization. We both found writing and presenting this paper together a significant experience. Ruby's perspective helped me to understand how deep the feelings among Indians run against being the subjects of study and in favor of Indian people's representing themselves. The questions of the power to do research and to control research findings took center stage as we described the investigative process from our respective positions. I would write a passage on the ethnographic study from my perspective, and she would write about it from hers. During our presentation, Ruby wept about indignities that researchers had caused her people over the years. My collaboration with Ruby deeply influenced me as I began work on a new edition of this book that would bring Native perspectives more clearly into focus.

Another experience also caused me to reflect on the original edition. I recently co-organized an art exhibition at the Tang Teaching Museum and Art Gallery of

Skidmore College with curator Ian Berry. The exhibition was titled "Staging the Indian: The Politics of Representation." It featured thirty-five photographs taken by Edward S. Curtis for his monumental series *The North American Indian.* We hung the Curtis prints alongside new works by six contemporary Native artists, made in response to Curtis's images. The artists used clay, paint, video, and still photography; some created elaborate installation pieces. Some of the works were rich with humor and irony, others with seriousness and beauty. Marcus Amerman (Choctaw), Judith Lowery (Mountain Maidu–Hamawi Pit River), James Luna (Luiseño), Nora Naranjo-Morse (Tewa), Shelley Niro (Bay of Quinte Mohawk), and Bently Spang (Tsistsistas) all contributed to the exhibition. Four of them spent a week in residence at Skidmore installing their work, giving students opportunities to interact informally with the visiting artists. All the artists also wrote essays for a book documenting the exhibition (Sweet and Berry 2002). The entire project helped me think further about issues of representation and ultimately colored how I looked back at the original edition of this book.

I asked myself whether I had represented the Tewas with respect. Had I honored their requests to omit sensitive material? Had I written the book in a way that could benefit them in their dealings with tourists? After several close readings, I believe that the answer to those questions is for the most part yes. I also asked myself whether I managed to pitch the book to the generalist without unnecessary academic jargon. Again, I believe that the answer is yes. But what the first edition lacks is the perspective of Native people. In an attempt to remedy this shortcoming, I include in this edition a new epilogue presenting more commentary from Indians about the dances and the act of dancing.

There is another issue that troubles me and needs clarification. The first edition includes photographs that my former husband, Roger Sweet, took during my fieldwork in 1973 and 1974. He took all of the photographs after we purchased photo permits from the appropriate village officials. Most of the images are group shots in which individuals are not highlighted, but six are close-ups of individual dancers, intended to illustrate ideas, not persons. Like Curtis in *The North American Indian,* I did not identify the subjects by name.

My failure to identify the dancers in the photographs reflects both my methodological assumptions at the time and the fact that I began my studies of Pueblo dance at a particularly conservative, non–Tewa-speaking village where no one wanted his or her name to appear in any of my writings. People feared that their neighbors might think they had given away sacred or private information. As a result, I decided to move my study north to the Tewa villages, where people were more open and even felt honored by the idea of a book about their dance traditions. Nevertheless, almost ten years passed between the time my husband took the photographs at the Tewa villages for my use in movement analysis and the time I began to consider using them as illustrations in a book. At that point, I continued to assume that individuals would not want their names to appear in print. Consequently, and in the tradition of early ethnographers and photographers like Edward Curtis, I did not name the Indians in the photographs. Neither did I name the four people who spent the most time teaching me about Tewa music and dance. As I worked on the second edition, Gary Roybal of San Ildefonso, John Garcia of Santa Clara, and Andy Garcia of San Juan encouraged me to try to contact and name the unidentified Tewas who taught me or who were featured in the photographs. This process was challenging but also rewarding because it took me back into the field to talk again with the people behind these beautifully powerful and resilient dance traditions.

As I ventured out to the Tewa villages in search of friends who might help me identify the people in the photographs, I thought about how the villages had changed since my first visits in the 1970s. One dramatic development has been population growth. In 1985, I reported that the population for the six Tewa villages ranged from as many as 1,486 persons at the largest village, San Juan, to as few as 107 at the smallest village, Pojoaque. Since then, according to the 2000 United States Census, all six villages have shown population increases. Between 1990 and 2000, the gains included a 29.5 percent increase at San Juan, where the total population rose to 6,748; a 25.8 percent increase at Nambe, where the population reached 1,764; and a 15.6 percent gain at Tesuque, where the total population was reported to be 806. For comparative purposes, census data for 1990 and 2000 in the nearby metropolitan area of Santa Fe show a 26.1 percent

So often Native people are thought of in stereotypical ways as having a connection with nature. Putting Indians in more contemporary dress, doing things that are more bourgeois and mundane, putting them in cars and gambling situations, decontextualizes that noble savage. It is more like Indians are just people. They drink, they smoke, act hurt, and do stupid things too. *Indian Gaming* takes the oftentimes romanticized image of Native people and makes it more mundane, putting them in everyday, almost boring, ludicrous situations, like the overweight guy who is chain—smoking as he plays the bingo machines.—Mateo Romero

Figure 2. Indian Gaming © *1996 by Mateo Romero, mixed media, 48 x 72.*

population increase. The increase in Santa Fe reflects the continuing attractive-ness of this "sunbelt" metropolitan area for large numbers of newcomers. Many of them came to the area first as tourists. Some returned to settle as retirees, adding to the growing numbers of non-Indians who are drawn to the Tewa vil-lages to witness the dances and purchase Native art.

Related to the increases in Tewa population numbers are tribal investments in casinos and associated tourist facilities on reservation land. At the time of this writing, four of the six Tewa villages have opened casino complexes, some complete with hotels, restaurants, bowling alleys, and golf courses. They are Pojoaque's Cities of Gold Casino, San Juan's Ohkay Casino, Santa Clara's Big Rock Casino, and Tesuque's Camel Rock Casino. These Tewa-owned businesses represent four of the eleven New Mexico casinos, all of which are located on Indian land, where they are relatively free from state gaming regulations. It is telling that the communities with the casinos show the greatest population growth, with the exception of Nambe, which has invested instead in a 150-acre industrial park, a fuel terminal, a warehouse that serves the Santa Fe Opera, and a recycling center. The population of Santa Clara has not jumped dramatically yet, but its casino is only a year old at the time I write. When asked why the pop-ulation figures have risen so, employees at the tribal governors' offices replied that job opportunities at the casinos and the possibility of sharing the profits have brought people home.

Although it is too soon to tell what the long-term impact of these casinos will be on the Tewas, it is hard to imagine that this will be anything less than signif-icant as new sources of income and new opportunities for employment become available. But the pueblos have taken steps to limit the effects of the casino on the community in other ways. All of the Tewa casinos are located outside the vil-lages proper—near the highways and on the outskirts of reservation land. As a result, the casinos do not disrupt the public village ritual performances, which continue to be held in the plazas of all the Tewa villages. The Tewas do not use the casinos as settings for ritual or theatrical presentations. Indeed, on August 12, 2001, Santa Clara's Big Rock Casino closed for the day because that is the day when the village's ritual dances and feasting take place. The marquee over the casino announced that it was closed in honor of Saint Clare and the Santa Clara feast day activities. The other casinos report that they do not close for village feast days, and in 2002 the management of the Santa Clara casino decided to join the others by staying open on August 12.

Debates have taken place in the local and national news media about the wisdom of opening casinos on Indian land. Some Tewa villages, such as San Ildefonso, have decided at this point not to engage in this type of development. The nearby Navajo Nation, the largest Indian reservation in the United States, has voted twice against the tribe's getting into the gaming business. Opinions about Indian casinos range from general moral indignation and resentment over the tribes' exemption from gaming regulations to applause for their potential economic success and their function as a step toward tribal self-sufficiency. One of my students reported that after giving her fifth-grade class a history lesson on the sixteenth-century Spanish conquistadores' destructive search for the Seven Cities of Gold, one youngster raised his hand to suggest that with modern casinos, the Indians were finally benefiting from that drive for fabulous wealth!

What has not changed since the writing of the first edition is considerable, too. Most importantly, the Tewas still remember, respect, and participate in their traditional cycle of dance events. Furthermore, they continue to see these occasions as essential for their communities' unity and well-being. The tribal governments continue to announce in the local media that many dance events are open to the public. They do not announce other dances, but visitors who happen on them may stay and watch as long as they abide by village rules. Still other events are strictly closed to outsiders. As greater numbers of tourists visit the villages each year, the Tewas continue to insist that those visitors abide by their rules for respectful observation (see, for example, Sweet 1989 and 1991).

A distinct separation between village ritual dances and theatrical performances held outside the villages, which I discuss at some length later in the book, also persists. The Anglo-organized Gallup Inter-Tribal Indian Ceremonial continues to be held annually, with 2002 marking its eighty-first year of operation. The Gallup event includes Indian dances, and in 2002 the organization's website stated, "The dance performances offer the opportunity for photos unobtainable anywhere else in the world." A San Juan Tewa dance group organized by San Juan resident, drummer, and singer Robert Aquino continues to participate in the Gallup event. In addition, the annual Santa Fe Indian Market still includes dance segments organized by the Southwestern Association for Indian Arts (SWAIA). These Indian dance segments are still held in the patio behind the Palace of the Governors. What have disappeared are the divisive dance competitions of the 1920s.

The Tewa-organized ceremonials at Puye Cliffs have not been resurrected since 1982, when two Indian women were fatally struck by lightning as they watched the festivities. The Nambe Falls event has been held pretty regularly, but in 2002 it was cancelled because of extreme fire danger caused by drought. Nonetheless, there were plans to bring this Tewa-organized ceremonial back in 2003 if conditions improved. The Eight Northern Indian Pueblo Council (ENIPC) Artist and Craftsman Show, now in its thirty-first year, continues to be held annually on the third weekend in July. Beginning in 2003, however, the ENIPC event will no longer rotate from village to village but will be held every

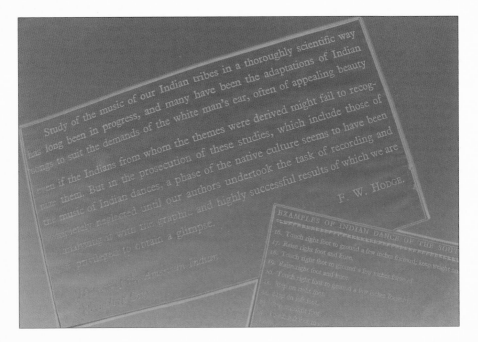

Figure 3. FW's Words © *by Nora Naranjo-Morse, monotype print; photograph by Gregory S. Morse.*

Anthropologist F.W. Hodge once wrote, "The study of the music of our Indian tribes in a thoroughly scientific way has long been in progress." I am always amazed at the weight of seemingly insignificant words such as the word "our" in the opening of his book.... Researchers like Mr. Hodge simply assumed their "thoroughly scientific" research allowed them ownership not only of information, but also the people who lived and safeguarded that information.

Hodge felt compelled and entitled to study his Indian tribe's music and dance with stick figures and step-by-step instruction. Nevertheless, the hidden nuances of a collective pause that only drummers and dancers hear and feel are things he was incapable of capturing.

Influenced by the idea of "research," I actually tried Hodge's step-by-step dance instructions, but by instruction line #17, I was lost and totally befuddled as to what dance I was doing and why; forget about trying to keep in mind the actual significance of the dance. Was that right foot down close to the ground or left foot up?—Nora Naranjo-Morse

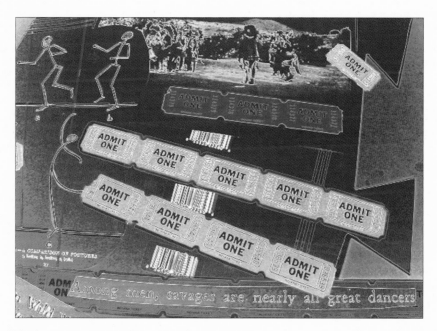

Figure 4. Among Men © *by Nora Naranjo-Morse, monotype print; photograph by* Gregory S. Morse.

Being a research subject is tricky business, especially now when what is left of Native culture has become such a commodity. Being someone's subject matter may be profitable, and for many, culturally validating. Who doesn't want their fifteen minutes of fame by having his or her experience documented? However, in Pueblo thought, the act of committing oneself to a dance is a single decision, a private decision, and ultimately a religious decision. Mr. Hodge simply did not understand this about his Native people and their music and dance.

—Nora Naranjo-Morse

year at San Juan Pueblo in a newly constructed permanent location. Although the main emphasis is on the arts and crafts, dance segments remain part of this all-Indian-run event.

Another place where visitors can see displays of dance segments is the Indian Pueblo Cultural Center (IPCC) in Albuquerque. Performances are scheduled throughout the day on most Saturdays and Sundays. Dancers also perform at the Indian Village of the New Mexico State Fairgrounds in Albuquerque each September.

The IPCC now has a website (www.indianpueblo.org/ipcc/) that features a brief description of the nineteen pueblos, including information about regularly held, open village dances. Contacting each village's tribal governor's office by telephone is still the best way to learn about upcoming open dances. At the time of this writing, the tribal governors' offices do not yet have their own websites. However, the ENIPC, which includes the six Tewa villages plus Taos and Picuris, began putting out an informative visitor's guide that includes essays by Tewa writers in 2000. Some of these essays feature insider observations about the dances. The ENIPC visitor guides were funded in part by the New Mexico Office of Indian Affairs and the Department of Tourism. Interested individuals may obtain copies by writing to Post Office Box 969, San Juan Pueblo, New Mexico, 87566, or by telephoning 1-800-793-4955.

Some semiprofessional Tewa dance groups who participate in theatrical displays still exist, but their membership seems to be in flux. The San Juan Indian Youth Dancers, for example, are no longer connected to the Alateen organization but are made up of twelve to fourteen friends and family members of Andy Garcia, the group's organizer and former governor of San Juan Pueblo. The group now calls itself the Tewa Dancers from the North, and its schedule depends on opportunities to perform. Andy Garcia's business card lists the group's repertoire as including the Buffalo dance, Eagle dance, Butterfly dance, Women's Special dance, Hopi-Tewa Deer dance, and Winter Buffalo dance. Another Tewa dance group that has attracted considerable attention lately is the Darren Rock Youth Dance Group, under the direction of Jeromy Yepa of Santa Clara Pueblo. John Garcia, also of Santa Clara Pueblo, states that the efforts of these young dancers will help maintain the ancient dance traditions well into the twenty-first century.

What follows this preface is the original text presented in its entirety as an artifact of ethnographic research conducted more than thirty years ago. Next is the new epilogue, where I present images and words by contemporary Pueblo Indians who regularly dance in village ritual events and who are willing to share their thoughts about dancing. The closing essay also offers the names of dancers unidentified in the original book and some tales of trying to locate and identify people in the photos. Finally, I finish this new edition with an account of a moment when cultural differences dissolved in an exchange of human concern, caring, and mutual respect in the emergency room of Santa Fe's St. Vincent Hospital. In this unlikely place, I came to realize that what really matters most about doing ethnography is the people who let outsiders into their world, are willing to teach them about that world, and, in a few cases, even let them into their hearts.

A 2002 School of American Research Summer Residency and the Ethel-Jane Bunting Foundation supported my work on this second edition. I would also like to thank Michael Ennis-McMillan for reading earlier drafts of the new material and Bruce Bernstein, John Garcia, and Gary Roybal for helping me to identify individuals in the original photographs. In addition, I need to thank Wendy Leighton for her research assistance. Finally, I wish to express my gratitude to Nora Naranjo-Morse and Mateo Romero for their poignant words and art.

Figure 5. Chorus:, *by Oqwa Pi (Abel Sanchez), c. 1930. School of American Research collections.*

PREFACE
TO THE FIRST EDITION

My interest in Tewa Pueblo Indian performance began in December of 1972, when I was a student of dance at the University of California, Irvine, visiting the Southwest between academic terms. The high point of my trip was a Pueblo Indian ritual performance honoring Christ on Christmas Eve in a crowded adobe village church. Never before had I witnessed such a powerful ritual event with so many elaborately costumed people dancing and singing en masse. My previous experience with dance lay in performing, choreographing, and teaching ballet and modern and jazz dance—all Western theatrical traditions that are important only to a small percentage of the people in my society. In contrast, the dance of the Pueblo Indians appeared to be necessary and vital for the entire Pueblo community. I left the performance with an overwhelming sense of reverence, respect, and admiration.

Returning to my courses at Irvine with a desire to know more about Pueblo Indian performance, I read everything I could find on Pueblo culture, and I prepared for fifteen months (June 1973 through September 1974) of fieldwork in New Mexico. At the end of that first period of fieldwork, I wrote a master's thesis on Pueblo Indian dance (Sweet 1975).

In 1975, I began to study cultural anthropology at the University of New Mexico. Throughout my graduate training in anthropology, I continued to attend Pueblo performances and to interview Pueblo Indian consultants, especially at the six Tewa Pueblo villages. Then, in 1979, as a Weatherhead Fellow and resident scholar at the School of American Research, I wrote my Ph.D. dissertation on Tewa performance (Sweet 1981). This book is based on portions of that dissertation, but rewritten primarily for the generalist and the southwestern traveler.

While Tewa village rituals are frequently called "dances" by the Tewas and their visitors, I speak of "dances" only to indicate particular forms such as the basket dance or the turtle dance. I refer to the larger ritual, which may include one or more dances, as a performance or an event, because private religious acts, songs, costumes, and feasting are equally important elements. For example, the Comanche dance and the buffalo dance are referred to as part of the San Juan feast day ritual performance or event. Details of Tewa religion are not presented in this book because the Pueblo Indians are very reluctant to discuss sacred religious matters with outsiders. I have therefore included only a general outline of their religious beliefs.

Throughout the book, I use the term "Anglo" to designate the non-Hispanic Caucasian population. In the Southwest, "Anglo" is commonly used in a general sense to indicate all people of European descent, except Hispanics. I decided to use "Anglo" in this way because of its wide colloquial acceptance and because I have not yet found a more satisfactory term. In addition, the word "theater" in this book means the performance tradition of Western, post-industrial societies. In chapter 3, ritual and theater are described as two extremes of a continuum rather than as a simple dichotomy.

Illustrative quotes are transcribed verbatim from interview tapes in order to ensure accuracy of interpretation. Grammatical errors reflect informal speech patterns and the fact that English is a second language for some consultants.

Since this book is written primarily for the generalist, references to other sources have been kept to a minimum for unencumbered reading. If no reference is cited after information is presented, the reader can assume that the information is widely expressed and generally accepted in the literature or it was observed by me during the fieldwork conducted between 1973 and 1981. Specialists who seek more detailed referencing should consult my dissertation (Sweet 1981).

The generosity of the Weatherhead Foundation and the School of American Research supported the research on which this book was based. I especially want to thank Douglas W. Schwartz and the staff at the School of American Research for making my year there productive and pleasurable. The Frieda Butler Foundation and the New Mexico State Health and Environment Department provided grants that made possible the use of video, film, and photography in my research.

I would also like to thank Philip K. Bock, Alfonso Ortiz, and Marta M. Weigle, who spent many hours discussing my research and writing. Thanks also to Allegra Fuller Snyder, who taught me so much about non-Western dance, and to Joann Kealiinohomoku, Luther Lyon, and Virginia Robicheau, who read and commented on earlier drafts of this book. Luther Lyon was particularly helpful in sharing his ideas and showing me unpublished fieldnotes and historical documents from his files. I am also grateful to Beatrice Chauvenet, Tom Dozier, Hester Jones, Marjorie Lambert, Ruth Montgomery, Lucille Stacey, and the late Margaret Moses, all of whom were particularly helpful with details about early Indian Detours and the first ceremonials.

To the many Tewa people who welcomed me into their homes, sat and talked with me, explained song texts, and showed me dance movements, I extend my gratitude and affection.

Figure 6. A young woman from the Tewa village of Santa Clara takes her place for a performance of the basket dance. She wears a traditional, hand-woven, black manta-dress and white shawl. (Photo by Roger Sweet, 1974.)

CHAPTER ONE

SEEKERS OF LIFE

The dancers file out of the kiva and move slowly into the village plaza to perform. Sounds of deep male voices singing, the clatter of deer hoof rattles, and the steady, resonant beat of the drum draw the Tewa people from their homes. Parrot feathers, embroidered dance kilts, striped blankets, and fringed shawls color the event. The people have come together for dancing, singing, and feasting; they will leave with a sense of renewal. The Tewa Pueblo Indians say that they dance and sing to "find new life," to "regain life," or to "seek life."

Visitors may find a Tewa village ritual performance in progress during any season of the year. In winter, the public performances tend to focus on hunting and game animal themes, while spring, summer, and fall events center on agriculture. The number of public ritual performances held annually varies from village to village and year to year. At San Ildefonso, San Juan, and Santa Clara, it is not uncommon for the people to hold six to ten public performances in one year; Nambe and Tesuque generally hold fewer, and Pojoaque currently has only one village performance each year.

For most events, long parallel lines of dancers move in unison to the beat of one or more drums (fig. 7). The dancers sing as they dance, or a chorus of male singers stands close by the dancers and accompanies them. These public performances often last from sunrise to sunset, demanding great endurance from performers who range in age from three years to over eighty. Each ritual occasion is the united expression of an entire Tewa community and helps reinforce Tewa Pueblo Indian traditions.

Figure 7. Led by a man carrying a banner, two long lines of dancers file into the plaza at San Ildefonso to begin the harvest dance. A chorus and a drummer accompany them. Each woman wears a wooden tablita headdress. (Photo by Roger Sweet, 1973.)

Not all who witness Tewa ritual performances understand or appreciate them. Some of the sixteenth- and seventeenth-century Spanish explorers and missionaries saw these events as devil worship and described Pueblo religion as idolatrous, its rituals dangerous to the souls of participants and observers. The Spanish missionaries were particularly disturbed by ritual performances involving masks, which they interpreted as blatant idol worship. One missionary referred to the masked dances as "an offering of the fruits of the earth to the Devil" (quoted in Bandelier 1937:207). Another tried to stop a masked ritual performance by walking through the plaza "with a cross upon his shoulders, a crown of thorns and a rope about his neck, beating his naked body" (Bandelier 1937:184).

In 1846, when the Tewas and other Pueblo Indians became a concern of the United States government, their ritual performances were described by some Anglos as immoral, pagan, repugnant, or simply a hindrance to the civilizing process. In the 1920s, Charles H. Burke, the United States commissioner of

Indian affairs, attempted to stop many forms of Indian ritual performance, claiming that these events contained "barbaric features" and interfered with family and farming responsibilities. The commissioner and the Protestant missionary groups who supported him failed to understand that many Indian ritual events are held specifically to unify families and ensure agricultural success. Burke's crusade against Indian ritual performances failed primarily because of protests voiced by both Indian and Anglo supporters of Pueblo religious freedom (Philip 1977:55–70).

While Burke was attempting to ban Indian rituals, Anglo businessmen in the Southwest saw Tewa and other Pueblo performances as potential tourist attractions. These entrepreneurs discovered that tourists would pay for guided trips to village ritual events and that Pueblo Indians could be brought into Southwestern towns to perform segments of their rituals for large groups of paying tourists. The Tewa Indians, however, discouraged Anglo businessmen from any serious attempts to convert their village rituals into tourist shows. Tourist performances do exist today, but these events, in which the Tewas present short segments of their native dances, have developed independently from the Tewa ritual cycle and stand as separate, tourist-oriented theatrical productions held outside the sacred village dance plazas. In spite of the pressures from Spanish and Protestant missionaries and Anglo government officials, Tewa village ritual performances survive. The people still dance and sing "to find new life."

Tewa Pueblo Indians

Contemporary Pueblo Indians are the proud descendents of native peoples who inhabited what is now the American Southwest as long ago as two millenia. By 500 B.C., these ancestors were living in small villages and growing corn, beans, and squash. Between A.D. 900 and 1300, prehistoric Pueblo peoples built elaborate towns with spectacular architecture, the most dramatic examples of which are the famous sites of Mesa Verde and Chaco Canyon. By the beginning of the fourteenth century, some of the Pueblos' ancestors had migrated to the Rio Grande Valley and established farming communities there.

In 1540, Francisco Vasquez de Coronado led the first European expedition into Pueblo territory. With several hundred armed men and five Franciscan missionaries, Coronado traveled northward from present-day Mexico in search of gold and converts. Soon the Pueblo Indians were declared Spanish subjects and introduced to Catholicism. This was a difficult period for the Pueblos because colonial Spanish policies were harsh. Civil and church authorities confiscated native religious paraphernalia, burned kivas (ceremonial chambers), and punished uncooperative Indians with public whippings, head shavings, and occasionally the amputation of a foot or hand. In 1665, Hopi Pueblo Indians reported that a priest whipped an Indian for practicing idolatry, then doused him with turpentine and set him on fire. During this same period, a Taos Pueblo woman was allegedly killed by a priest because she failed to spin cotton for him (Simmons 1979:184).

By 1680, Pueblo resentment of the Spaniards became so great that the Indians united in revolt, driving their oppressors out of the area. The Spaniards returned thirteen years later, however, to reestablish control, though after the reconquest their treatment of the Pueblo Indians became less harsh. The Spaniards continued to rule Pueblo lands until 1821, when the newly independent Mexican government took control. Twenty-seven years later, the area became a territory of the United States. Throughout these political changes, the Pueblo Indians attempted to live their lives as their ancestors had for centuries.

Modern Pueblo Indian villages can be identified by location and language, the languages being Hopi, Zuni, Keresan, Tiwa, Towa, and Tewa. Hopi-speaking Pueblo Indians, the westernmost group, inhabit villages in northern Arizona, and Zuni Pueblo lies near the Arizona–New Mexico border (fig. 8). In New Mexico, the Pueblo Indians living in the villages of Acoma, Laguna, Santa Ana, Zia, San Felipe, Cochiti, and Santo Domingo all speak the Keresan language. Tiwa speakers are found at the geographically scattered villages of Isleta, Sandia, Picuris, and Taos, while Towa is spoken only in the village of Jemez. Finally, Tewa-speaking people, the subjects of this book, live in the villages of Tesuque, Nambe, Pojoaque, San Ildefonso, Santa Clara, and San Juan, all within a twenty-mile stretch of land along the Rio Grande and its tributaries, north of Santa Fe, New Mexico. Population figures for the Tewa villages range from as many as 1,487 inhabitants at San Juan to as few as 107 at Pojoaque (Simmons 1979:221).

The traditional economy of the Tewas, like that of all Pueblo Indians, emphasized agriculture along with hunting and trading. Today, some Tewa families still farm the irrigated lands surrounding their villages, and the men occasionally go on hunting trips. Most contemporary Tewa families, however, depend on wage work and/or sales of arts and crafts. Some Tewa people commute to jobs in Santa Fe, while others temporarily leave their villages to work in other states. More Tewa Indians are attending colleges and universities and then taking professional positions in their own villages and elsewhere.

Visitors often find the Tewa villages aesthetically appealing. Many Anglo artists and architects are inspired by the simple adobe houses that surround the village plazas, by the kivas with their ladders reaching toward the sky, and by the massive mission churches with heavy wooden doors (fig. 9). Traditional Tewa houses, usually located in the central part of the village, have flat roofs supported by pine logs, or *vigas*. Inside, there is often a corner fireplace, and near

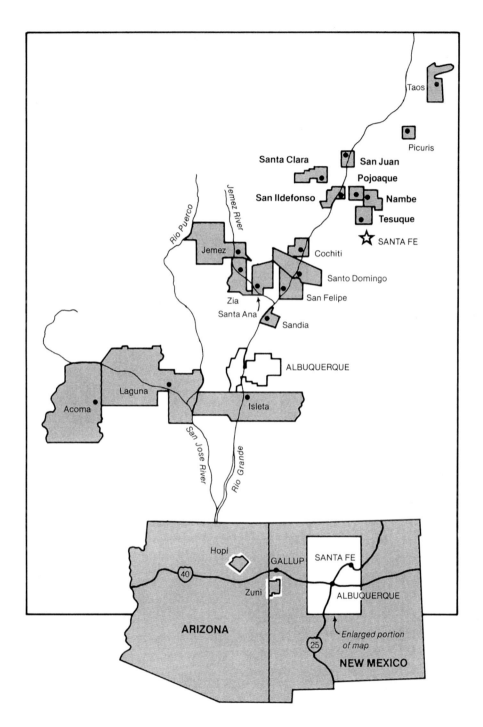

Figure 8. Locations of the modern Pueblo Indian lands and villages. (Map by Carol Cooperrider.)

Figure 9. In front of the village church, San Ildefonso Tewas present the Comanche dance to honor their patron saint. (Photo by Roger Sweet, 1973.)

the house there may be a beehive-shaped adobe oven used to bake bread, cakes, and cookies. The newer houses built at the outer edges of the villages are ranch-style homes similar to those in any modest American housing development. Many are constructed of concrete blocks and wood rather than of the traditional adobe bricks. Both old and new homes are filled with contemporary furniture, often including a stereo and a television. Frequently, the interior walls are decorated with Navajo rugs, Mexican shawls, Hopi or Apache baskets, photographs of family members, and pictures of Christ or a favorite saint.

Some Tewa villages have one large plaza; others have as many as four smaller ones. These open spaces are not paved, partly because the ritual performances are held in these areas and performer contact with the earth is symbolically important. In villages with several plazas, the ritual dancing is often repeated in each area as the dancers make a circuit through the village.

Tewa kivas may be round or square, semisubterranean or at ground-level. Some are entered by ascending a ladder or stairway to the roof and then descending a second ladder through a ceiling opening down to the kiva floor (fig. 10). Others are entered through doors at ground level. Tewa kivas may stand isolated in the plaza or be integrated into a village house block. At the village of San Ildefonso, visitors can see an example of both an isolated round kiva with a stairway entrance and an integrated square kiva with a ground-level doorway. All Tewa kivas are constructed of adobe and carefully maintained.

Kivas are the scenes of preparation for village rituals: both men and women participants practice for their performance inside the kiva. When a public performance is to begin, the participants move from the kiva to the dance plaza, symbolizing the Tewa origin myth that describes how the first people emerged from a world below this one (Ortiz 1969:37). Private rituals not performed for the public also take place in the kivas, which are off-limits to all non-Indian visitors.

Kivas are not the only religious buildings to be found in Tewa villages; each also owns and maintains a Catholic church. Some Tewas regularly attend mass, while others seldom go. In the past, the Tewa people may have seen the Church as a threat to their traditional religious beliefs and practices, but today they seem comfortable having two religious systems coexist within their villages. Indeed, church walls may even be decorated with native motifs such as birds, corn, or cloud symbols.

Some visitors also become intrigued by the social organization of Tewa villages. The moiety system, a division of the people into two major groups, is central to traditional Tewa social organization. Typically, each member of a Tewa village belongs to either the "summer people," associated with the south, femininity, and plant life, or to the "winter people," associated with the north, masculinity, and minerals (see Ortiz 1969). Each Tewa belongs to his or her father's moiety, although in some cases a woman may change to her husband's moiety. The moiety system is sometimes expressed publicly during ritual performances as each group presents a different dance, uses its own kiva, or performs in its own plaza area.

A native priest heads each moiety and directs ritual activities for half the year. These priests are aided by war captains, who, together with their assistants, are most visibly in charge of the village performances. They watch over the events to make sure that visitors maintain a respectful distance from the dancers, stay away from the kivas, and observe photography and sound-recording rules. The war captains' group is also instrumental in selecting dancers and singers and organizing dance practices.

Each Tewa village also has a council consisting of the current governor and his lieutenants, all previous governors, and the male heads of native religious societies. First established by the Spaniards in the belief that the Pueblo Indians lacked a legitimate political structure, the offices of governor and lieutenant governor—perhaps because of their foreign origin—are responsible for any secular

Figure 10. After a performance of the yellow corn dance, Nambe Tewas return to their semi-subterranean kiva by climbing the steps and then descending a ladder. (Photo by Roger Sweet, 1974.)

matters brought to the council, as well as dealings with government officials and other people from outside the Tewa world.

The Tewas' native religious system focuses primarily on group rather than individual concerns. Religious activities seek group harmony and community health and promote seasonal changes and weather control more often than they mark changes in an individual's status or celebrate personal religious experiences. As an extension of this concern for group welfare, the Tewas honor animals and plants that are part of their environment, seeking a harmonious coexistence with the natural world.

Fundamental to Tewa religion are the many supernaturals who can use their power either constructively or destructively. One important type of supernatural is called *okhua* by the Tewas but is more commonly known to non-Tewas by the Hopi Pueblo term *kachina*. Okhua or kachinas are sometimes described as spirits of the dead. Only people who have devoted their lives to religious activities, however, will join the kachinas after death (Ortiz 1969:96). In private ritual performances, men who have been ritually initiated embody the kachina spirits, which may be male or female mythical characters, animals, insects, or plants. Kachina dancers wear elaborate masks that hide their human identity even from Tewa women and children. It was the masked kachina dances that especially troubled the early Spanish missionaries, and probably for that reason, Tewa kachina dances are no longer open to the public. No outsiders are allowed to witness these most sacred performances, and the Tewas will not speak to visitors about the masked beings or their ritual appearances.

Historically, the Tewa Indians had several esoteric religious societies that were responsible for performing specific rites during the annual ritual cycle. There were societies of medicine men, hunters, warriors, women, and, the most visible and interesting to visitors, the *kossa* ("k'ohsaa") clowns. The current state of these societies is difficult to determine because they are not openly discussed with outsiders. Apparently, some societies no longer function in Tewa villages, but the kossa clowns of San Juan and San Ildefonso are, without question, still active (fig. 11). Their numbers are few, but they dedicate themselves to the spiritual and ritual life of the village, and, like members of all the religious societies, they must be instructed in highly esoteric matters and ritually initiated for life. They supervise some of the public performances and engage in ritual buffoonery, reversing and inverting reality by doing things incorrectly or backwards. Thus, they help reinforce socially acceptable behavior by demonstrating what is unacceptable, using pantomime, speech, or ridicule of people who have broken Tewa social norms. Anglo visitors are not exempt from the antics of these clowns, who may target an unsuspecting tourist for one of their pranks.

Two Types of Public Performance

The village rituals that are the public aspects of the Tewa religious system are regular parts of the Tewa ritual calendar. With their dramatic action, dance, and music, these traditional performances are communal public prayers presented primarily for those who understand and share the Tewa language, beliefs, and worldview. Each year, some Tewas also participate in a second type of performance: theatrical productions that are generally held away from the village for non-Tewa audiences. Anglo-organized ceremonials, Tewa-organized ceremonials, and arts and crafts fairs are the most elaborate of these productions and have been the most popular and regularly held since the 1920s. Although participation in theatrical productions is regarded as enjoyable, this second category of public performance is not considered as important for the Tewa community as is performing in a village ritual.

During the first quarter of this century, when Southwestern towns began to compete for the tourist trade, local businesses and chambers of commerce started promoting commercial shows called *ceremonials,* in which "Indians were hired to perform for the Anglo tourists whose presence in the town promoted the local interests" (Vogt 1955:820). These theatrical productions encouraged tourists to stay in town a few days and spend money while being entertained by Indians participating in sports competitions and music and dance performances. Gallup, Santa Fe, and Albuquerque hosted the early Anglo-organized ceremonials in which the Tewas most often took part.

After years of experience in Anglo-organized ceremonials, the Tewas began to design and organize their own. Adopting some of the Anglo entrepreneurs' ceremonial practices and rejecting others, the Tewas developed tourist-oriented events that creatively combined ritual and theater practices. Santa Clara Pueblo held the first of these Tewa-organized ceremonials at Puye Cliffs, ten miles from the village; it continued as an annual event from 1957 until 1982. In 1961, the Nambe Tewas established the Nambe Falls ceremonial, which is still held each year.

Today, both Anglo- and Tewa-organized ceremonials have become rare, while arts and crafts fairs have gained in popularity, perhaps because they more directly address Tewa commercial interests. Some fairs are organized by Anglos and others by Indian groups, but they share an emphasis on displays, demonstrations, and sales of arts and crafts. Performances of Indian dance and music are secondary attractions usually held off to the side of the main sales booth area. Of the many Indian arts and crafts fairs held throughout the Southwest, the one that most directly involves the Tewas is the Eight Northern Indian Pueblo Council (ENIPC) Artist and Craftsman Show.

Ceremonials and Indian arts and crafts fairs, as commercial theatrical productions designed for non-Indians, are events that simultaneously unite and separate the Indian and the visitor. They bring Tewa Indians and Anglo tourists together to share and experience a combination of the two cultures' performance traditions. At the same time, these events set the two groups apart by delineating and highlighting their cultural differences. Thus, Tewa Indian performers and Anglo observers both can experience a combining of cultural elements into a new form, as well as a reinforcing of cultural boundaries.

New Life

All Tewa performances, ritual or theatrical, express a central theme of finding or seeking new life, regaining or renewing life. While each dance or song carries specific meanings and stresses certain aspects of the Tewa world, all of them are underlain by this notion of seeking, finding, regaining, and renewing life. It is a recurrent and important theme that encompasses both individual and cultural rejuvenation or revitalization.

Tewa songs, gestures, and costumes incorporate many symbolic references to this theme of new life (see Laski 1959). The songs often refer to the dawn, youths, flowers, the growth of corn and other kinds of plants, and rain and signs of rain, such as clouds, thunder, lightning, and rainbows. To an agrarian society

Figure 11. Mountain Sheep Chasing the Koshare, *1951 by Alfonso Roybal, Awa Tsireh San Ildefonso Pueblo. 35372/13, Museum of Indian Arts and Culture/Laboratory of Anthropology, Musuem of New Mexico. www.miac.lab. Photograph by Blair Clark.*

living in an arid climate, these symbols promise the renewal of life that is inherent in natural cycles.

Dance gestures visually reinforce the symbolic power of the songs' images. An upward reaching of the arms with palms lifted suggests the welcoming of rain; lowering of the arms may indicate digging, planting, or harvesting new crops. Arc-like gestures from side to side can suggest rainbows and clouds. The dancers hold evergreens, rattles, baskets, or ears of corn symbolizing life and growth. After some Tewa ritual performances, the dancers raise the evergreens to their mouths and inhale, thus taking in new life from a plant that remains green and "alive" all year.

Costume designs also provide symbols of new life. The long tassels hanging from a sash suggest the blessing of rain drops; woven yarn headdresses depict the squash blossoms of spring; embroidered designs symbolize layers of clouds; and a fan of feathers or a basket may represent the power of the sun. No single meaning can be attributed to a Tewa costume, dance gesture, or song, but the many layers of meanings all revolve around the central notion of new life. Even the translations of the Tewa terms for private rituals performed by the native priests reflect this theme: for example, the priests perform "bringing the buds to life" in

February, "bringing the leaves to life" in March, and "bringing the blossoms to life" in April (Ortiz 1969:98–100).

Tewa ritual events as complete experiences exemplify new life because they are seen by the Tewa people as mechanisms for revitalizing the community and bringing it together again. If, in a world of changing values, individuals begin to lose sight of their roles as Tewa Indians or to forget Tewa beliefs, then sharing in a traditional village event or even a theatrical performance can renew feelings of identity. The performers can bring Tewa families and friends into contact and reawaken in them concepts central to the Tewa worldview.

Perhaps this idea of new life has helped the Tewas maintain their cultural distinctiveness throughout a history of contact with other Native American groups, as well as with Europeans and Anglo Americans. The community regularly regains its cultural life as members dance the ancient dances and sing the ancient songs in costumes that have not changed significantly since their grandparents and great-grandparents danced in the plazas. For the Tewas, seeking and regaining life is seeking and regaining a rich cultural heritage.

Figure 12. Young Santa Clara Pueblo dancers at a sno-cone booth between dance sets (Photo by Roger Sweet, 1973).

Figure 13. One of the most colorful Tewa dances is the Comanche dance, performed here by San Ildefonso Tewas. (Photo by Roger Sweet, 1973.)

CHAPTER TWO

TEWA VILLAGE RITUALS

Tewa village rituals bombard the senses. Through crowds of spectators, the visitor sees masses of rhythmically moving bodies arrayed in colorful costumes and paraphernalia (see fig. 13). Excited children run through the village, their laughter mingling with the voices of singers and the repetitive sounds of bells, rattles, and drums. The smells of freshly baked bread, burning piñon, and steaming stews permeate the air. Together, the careful ritual preparations, the group movement sequences, the closely interrelated dance and music, the costumes, and the audience itself create a performance that communicates important images and messages to performer and observer alike.

Some Tewas agree to dance and sing in the village rituals more often than others. Women may be needed at home to care for youngsters or cook food for feasting. Some people may be unable to take time off from their jobs. Though participating is seen as a community responsibility, no one individual is expected to dance in every ritual event. Those who choose not to sing or dance are still considered important participants in the ritual performance. There is no "audience" in the Western theatrical sense of the word because the Tewas do not passively watch the action but instead consider the role of dance watching to be one of active listening. Tewa audiences contribute their thoughts to the communal prayer that is dramatized by the singers and dancers.

The Performance

Each ritual event is part of an annual cycle of village performances, a cycle that reflects seasonal changes and the traditional subsistence activities associated with each season. Only certain dances can be performed in the spring, and others in the summer, winter, or fall. The village council, often referred to by the Tewas as the tribal council, usually selects the dances and dance dates, although a few specific dances must be requested by special groups. For example, at the village of San Juan, the unmarried men request the deer dance each year, and the women's society, the cloud or basket dance.

Once the dance and date are chosen, the war captains and their assistants ask the village composers to prepare the songs. The composers must recall traditional songs for some dances, such as the deer, yellow corn, Comanche, butterfly, and harvest dances, while for others, such as the turtle, cloud, and basket dances, they compose new songs each year. The war captains' group then requests the lead male singers—those considered most musically gifted—to meet and practice with the composers in the kiva. Later, the other male participants join this group for practice, and the dance steps are set. Again, for some dances, traditional movement patterns are recalled, and for others, new choreographic combinations are created.

Finally, the war captains' group invites the women participants to attend the practice sessions in the kiva. Assistant war captains go to the women's homes and make formal requests: "We have chosen you to enlighten us and to help us gain life" (Garcia and Garcia 1968:239). If the woman is married, they must speak to her in front of her husband, but the decision to take part is hers alone. If she is not married, the request must be made in front of her father, who usually gives his permission.

On the fifth night before the dance, an expedition of young men gathers the evergreens that will be worn or carried by the dancers. Traditionally, they walked many miles to the mountains, collected evergreen branches while praying, and carried them back to the village, all in one night. Today, pickup trucks may take the gatherers into the mountains, but the evergreens are still collected with reverence because they remain powerful symbols of life.

The length of the practice period varies, but four evenings in the kiva is commonest. Throughout the practice period, costumes and paraphernalia are prepared. On the evening of the performance, the participants may present a short prelude dance in the plaza. The next day, a final practice session may be held before emergence from the kiva.

Tewa dance style is formal, controlled, and repetitive, with relatively simple steps. The dancers move in unison, with torsos held erect and limbs close to the center of the body (fig. 14). Tewa dancers usually contract their elbows to about a ninety-degree angle and hold them four or five inches from the body. Most gestures are made through space in a flat arc, rather than in a straight line projecting out from the dancer's body.

Figure 14. In classic Tewa style, participants in the yellow corn dance at Nambe hold their bodies erect and arms close to their torsos. Men contract their knees slightly more than do women. (Photo by Roger Sweet, 1974.)

For most steps, the dancers contract their knees only slightly, so their feet remain close to the ground. The men usually lift their feet a bit higher than do the women. The *ântegeh* (from the Tewa "foot," *ân,* and "to lift," *tegeh*) is the most basic step in Tewa dance. Kurath and Garcia (1970:82) described it as "foot lifting with emphasis on right foot: upbeat of raising right knee while supporting weight on left foot; accented lowering of right foot, while raising left heel and slightly flexing knees; unaccented raising of right knee while lowering left heel." This step may be done in place or traveling forwards, sidewards, or diagonally.

Other common Tewa steps include a stylized deer walk and a buffalo walk. The deer dancer holds a cane-like stick in each hand and leans forward, bearing his weight on the sticks while bending his legs. He meanders slowly, creating the illusion of a four-legged animal (fig. 15). The buffalo walks upright in a gait that shifts the body weight from side to side, the knees bending deeply in a heavy, lumbering walk. Occasionally, the choreography calls for small jumps (springing from and landing on both feet), hops (springing from one foot and landing on the same foot), and small, low leaps (springing from one foot and landing on the other). Knee bends in place with weight on both feet are sometimes used, in addition to a shuffle step (see Kurath and Garcia [1970] for notation of these steps).

Figure 15. With blackened face and a headdress of antler and yucca stalks, a San Ildefonso deer dancer executes the stylized deer walk. (Photo by Roger Sweet, 1974.)

In the most sacred Tewa dances, a single file of men ântegeh in place, occasionally pivoting to change their facing direction. This choreographic pattern is considered to be the most sacred and is primarily associated with males because it is the same pattern found in the private kachina dances performed by men in the kivas. Other dances may take a double-file formation, especially when a large number of women participate. The lines usually alternate men and women, or a line of men faces one of women. Less frequently, the dance formation takes the form of a circle that typically rotates counterclockwise.

The performers usually follow a prescribed spatial circuit, repeating a five-verse dance set in each designated area. Sometimes they perform the final set of the circuit within the kiva, then after a short rest, return for another circuit through the village. There rarely are fewer than four, and sometimes as many as ten, circuits completed during the day, and some Tewa dances include extra prelude and postlude sections. A day of dancing often begins at dawn and lasts until sunset.

In any Tewa performance, music and dance are tightly interwoven. Each song is a prayer. More than mere accompaniment for the dancers, the songs are an integral part of the event, helping to communicate the meanings of the ritual. Ethnomusicologists have noted this interdependence in their work with Tewa song composers, who find it difficult to perform a song without also dancing or to comment on silent films of Tewa dance. Tewa women caring for infants or preparing food indoors can often describe the section of the dance in progress simply by hearing the music. Although most Tewa villages permit photography and even silent filming of their public performances, permission to make sound recordings is typically more difficult to obtain; songs are powerful and must be protected.

Only after the singers have learned the songs can the dancers begin their practice using the music to guide them through the choreography. The tempo of the music, of course, sets the dancers' speed. Usually, the tempo is constant, but in some cases, such as that of the San Juan cloud dance, a slow beat accelerates until it is very fast, then suddenly drops back once again, the dancers following suit. The tremolo, or rolling of drum or rattle, musical phrasing, and changes in the beat are techniques that cue the dancers to a change in facing direction or formation. A switch from the usual double beat to triple beat—called a t'an—often signals a slight hesitation in the ântegeh step.

Self-accompanied dances such as the San Juan turtle dance most dramatically express the relationship between music and movement. Here, the dancers are simultaneously the musicians as they ântegeh in place, each with a tortoiseshell rattle tied behind the right knee. The rattle sounds with each step, and the dancers sing as they move. Other percussion instruments used by male dancers include painted gourd hand rattles and commercially made sleigh bells sewn onto a leather belt. In addition, men who take the role of the buffalo in the buffalo dance wear kilts edged with rows of cone-shaped tin tinklers.

Figure 16. Five handsomely clad drummers produce a powerful beat for San Ildefonso singers and dancers. (Photo by Roger Sweet, 1973.)

The Tewas purchase or trade for drums, which are made from hollowed cottonwood tree trunks. Pueblo drum makers cover the ends with horse or bull hide and sometimes paint the body with bright colors. Drumsticks are carved from soft pine, and a stuffed hide ball is tied to one end. The best-known Pueblo drum makers are from the Keresan Pueblo village of Cochiti, where many Tewa drums originate.

Performers treat their drums with respect and sometimes give them names. After using a drum, the performers may ritually "feed" it with a sprinkle of cornmeal. The pitch of a drum can be altered by changing drumsticks or by turning it over and beating on the opposite end, changes that a good drummer can accomplish without losing a beat. The number of drummers varies with the dances from one to as many as four or five (fig. 16), and drummers often alternate during a long ritual performance.

Tewa performance costumes vary according to village, dance, and time of year, but there are some common elements in all costume designs (see Roediger 1961). The woman dancer generally wears a *manta*-dress, made of black or white wool or heavy cotton fabric and bordered with geometric patterns in green, black, and white embroidery (fig. 17). Under this heavier garment, she may wear a cotton shirt or dress trimmed in lace. A brightly colored, lace-trimmed shawl may be pinned at her right shoulder, and a red woven sash tied at her waist. For some dances, she will be asked to dance barefoot, and for others, to wear moccasins. Silver and turquoise necklaces, bracelets, and pins always decorate a woman's festive attire, and in some dances, a wooden or feather headdress adorns her head. The wooden headdresses, called *tablitas* (see fig. 7), can have elaborately carved or painted symbols of corn, clouds, or the sun. Frequently, a woman dancer carries evergreens, and sometimes ears of corn, in each hand.

A male dancer wears a white kilt with edges embroidered in red, green, and black. For some dances, his chest and legs are bare except for body paint, and for others, he wears a white shirt and crocheted leggings. At his waist, the male dancer usually wears bells, an embroidered sash, or a long-fringed white rain sash. He carries a gourd rattle in his right hand, along with evergreen sprigs, while in the left hand he holds only evergreens. Moccasins on the feet and usually a few feathers tied at the top of the head complete the man's costume.

Some Meanings and Messages

Tewa village ritual performances are rich with layers of symbolic meaning and messages encoded in songs, gestures, actions, costumes, and paraphernalia. Along with the central theme of new life, other important Tewa concepts find expression in ritual, including those of subsistence, society, beauty, space, time, and humor. Communication of these concepts is directed toward the performers themselves, toward fellow Tewas, and toward the supernaturals.

SUBSISTENCE, SOCIETY, AND BEAUTY

Subsistence themes ensure, celebrate, and give thanks for plant and animal life and for the rainfall essential to it. Because the Tewas traditionally depended upon agriculture and hunting, the importance of these messages cannot be overemphasized. Through performances, the people communicate statements about the abundance and fertility of plants and animals in their environment.

A key subsistence symbol is corn. For centuries a crucial and versatile food source, corn plays an important role in Tewa mythology, and all aspects of the plant are considered to be symbolically powerful. Its life cycle is seen as a paradigm of all other natural life cycles. Corn designs may be embroidered on a dancer's manta or carved in her wooden tablita headdress, and she often carries ears of corn in her hands. Tewas sprinkle cornmeal as they stand watching the village ritual performances, a sacred offering to the supernatural world. Corn and the related need for rain are central themes in many Tewa songs (Spinden 1933:95):

Figure 17. Dancing at the Puye Cliffs ceremonial, a Santa Clara woman wears a traditional white manta-dress, elaborately embroidered, and a lace-trimmed blue shawl over one shoulder. Her male counterpart wears a white kilt, crocheted leggings, a rain sash, and a yarn squash-blossom headdress. (Photo by Roger Sweet, 1974.)

Ready we stand in San Juan town,
Oh, our Corn Maidens and our Corn Youths!
Oh, our Corn Mothers and our Corn Fathers!

Now we bring you misty water
And throw it different ways
To the north, the west, the south, the east
To heaven above and the drinking earth below!

Then likewise throw your misty water
Toward San Juan!
Oh, many that you are, pour water
Over our Corn Maidens' ears!
On our Wheat Maidens
Thence throw you misty water,
All round about us here!

On Green Earth Woman's back
Now thrives our flesh and breath,
Now grows our strength of arm and leg,
Now takes form our children's food!

A second group of symbolic meanings expresses the social dimensions of the Tewa world. The performances make explicit and implicit statements about Tewa society, not only reflecting social roles, relationships, and responsibilities but also helping to establish, shape, and reinforce them. The village performances are arenas for demonstrating how the Tewas interact socially and what it means to be a member of Tewa society. During a performance, for example, an aunt might help a nephew prepare for his first deer dance. The women of a household will work together preparing a feast for dancers and visitors. A clown may ridicule a man because he neglects his family. Each of these acts makes public the Tewas' notions of social roles and responsibilities.

One of the more obvious statements of social responsibility that is expressed during many village rituals is the "throw," "giveaway," or "throwaway." People from the community bring out large baskets filled with fruit, packaged snack foods, candy, cigarettes, money, and even small household items such as towels, brooms, pots, and pans. These they throw out to the dancers and singers as a statement of community sharing. The performers catch or pick up the gifts as they continue to dance and sing. Relatives of the performers quickly take the gifts home so that the dance is not disrupted. Throws may also be directed toward the observers, both Indian and non-Indian. When this happens, there is often more laughter and scrambling for the goods. Non-Tewa visitors who catch items are expected to accept them as gifts.

The most fundamental social statement is communicated simply by the act of participating in a village ritual performance. When a Tewa decides to sing or dance in, or attend, a ritual performance, he or she demonstrates a commitment to being Tewa and contributes to the cohesiveness of the social group, which is distinguished from all "outsiders." Some Tewa Indians claim that to remain a Tewa, one must, in some capacity, participate in village performances (Ortiz 1979b: 287–298). As the Tewas participate, they make commitments of time, effort, and money to traditions and to the community. They may forfeit a few days' wages to spend the required time at practice. Their costumes may need costly and time-consuming repairs, and they must purchase and cook large quantities of food for feasting. Through participation, they are reminded of their cultural heritage and renew their strength to continue as members of Tewa society.

In addition to subsistence and society, Tewa conceptions of beauty are expressed during a village ritual performance. For the Tewas, beauty is found in the power of group movement, in repetitive and understated choreography and song composition, and in a serious, respectful, and dedicated performance. The motion of the entire group together is more important and more beautiful than the performance of any individual; there are no stars. Those who do stand out are criticized for being "too showy" or for dancing "too hard." A single dancer must not destroy the illusion of the group moving as one.

Group unity is facilitated, in part, by the repetitive or redundant nature of the dances and songs. Redundancy not only makes aesthetic expression predictable and familiar, producing a sense of pleasurable security, but also simplifies execution. By keeping the movement and song vocabulary relatively simple, and by recombining and repeating this vocabulary, a large group of non-specialists is more likely to dance and sing successfully in unison. Performance in unison not only is an aesthetic imperative but also reinforces a Tewa concern for the needs of the whole community over those of specific individuals.

Tewas see beauty in the subtle understatement of the dance performance. Gestures are typically close to the body, and steps are usually small progressions with little elevation. The women keep their eyes cast down and their manner demure and contained. This understated performance style also helps to keep any one individual from standing out from the group.

The Tewas also find beauty in songs. They admire their composers for their skill at creating new songs or remembering the traditional ones. The beauty of repetition and understatement are important aspects of Tewa songs. Singers also bring beauty to the ritual when they sing with strong, clear voices. Note the simple yet elegant use of metaphor in the following section of a Tewa song (Spinden 1933:94):

Oh our Mother the Earth, oh our Father the Sky,
Your children are we, and with tired backs
We bring you the gifts that you love.
Then weave for us a garment of brightness;
May the warp be the white light of morning,
May the weft be the red light of evening,
May the fringes be the falling rain,
May the border be the standing rainbow.
Thus weave for us a garment of brightness
That we may walk fittingly where birds sing,
That we may walk fittingly where grass is green,
Oh our Mother the Earth, oh our Father the Sky!

The beauty of the performance results from the concentration and commitment of the participants. Tewas speak of this as dancing and singing with respect, or "from the heart," which, as one Tewa man said, "makes the meaning straight." Another said, "You've got to concentrate a lot. Dance with your whole heart in it. Nothing else in your mind—just what is taking place there. Give it all you've got. Singing is the same way. When I sing, I sing from my heart up."

An example of the communication of all three themes—subsistence, society, and beauty—is the cloud dance, also called the corn maiden dance or the three times dance. It is unique among Tewa dances because each time the long line of male dancers appears, only two women participate with them. Eight women are selected for these roles, a different pair for each of the four appearances. They wear elaborate eagle feather headdresses and brightly colored shawls and carry an ear of corn in each hand. They travel with small steps in front of the line of men, who sing and step in place (fig. 18).

The cloud dance communicates many messages, but those about subsistence, society, and beauty are most obvious. Usually held in February, the dance is a reminder that the cold winter months are nearly over and spring, with its promise of new life, is near. The prominence of the women dancers expresses this message because Tewas associate femaleness with agriculture and warmth (Ortiz 1965:390). The ears of corn carried by the women underscore the theme of agriculture. The women's headdresses symbolize rainbows and clouds, both harbingers of the rain needed for crops, and cloud designs embroidered on the women's dresses also invoke rain.

The men's costumes reinforce the message of seasonal change and a new agricultural cycle. The long fringes on white sashes represent falling rain; tortoise shell knee rattles promote fertility; and evergreen branches symbolize life. One Tewa man described the sound of gourd rattles as "like the sound of summer showers."

Figure 18. This woman's modest style and obvious concentration convey Tewa notions of beauty during the San Juan cloud dance. (Photo by Roger Sweet, 1974.)

The social messages communicated during the cloud dance refer to the structure of Tewa society, carefully classifying the people who make up the village. Cloud dance songs typically mention all the leaders and social groups in the village, such as the women's societies, clown societies, moieties, and native priests. Ties between families and friends find public expression as, for example, an aunt pins a one, five, or twenty dollar bill on her niece's costume, a gesture of appreciation that can take place while the dancer is performing or between dance sets. In either case, the dancer maintains a serious expression and does not overtly acknowledge the gift. Pinning money becomes a public statement about personal relationships. While the cloud dance defines social groups and personal ties, a concomitant "throw" expresses community cohesiveness and social responsibility. As dancers, singers, and observers catch the tossed gifts, the notion of community support is made public.

The choreographic structure of the cloud dance epitomizes notions of beauty. The dancers begin each dance set by forming a long line, shoulder to shoulder; two women take positions near the ends of the line, and the lead singers stand in the middle. The whole line ântegeh in place, the movements of individuals subordinate to the powerful totality of the group. Slowly and unobtrusively, the two women move out from the line, face each other, and begin to move toward each other with small diagonal steps. They meet, pass, and continue traveling to the opposite ends of the line, then turn and travel back to their starting positions. They repeat this pattern again and again. Near the end of the dance set, each woman must be near her starting position so that she can slip back into her place in the line as a music cue directs her. Although the cloud dance highlights women, their movements remain small, with their eyes cast down, because those judged most beautiful are the women who contain their movements, appear demure, and dance "from the heart" with deep concentration and quiet dedication. Dancing "from the heart" also helps to unite participants with the supernaturals. The entire performance is a prayer to the supernatural world, the women dancers symbolizing the two corn mothers, central figures in the Tewa origin myth.

SPACE, TIME, AND HUMOR

The Tewa Indians give great importance to spatial definitions of their world. In ritual performances, this concern with space appears in frequent and persistent references to the four cardinal directions and their intersection. Through gesture and song, space is symbolically ordered and the Tewa world is spatially defined. Each direction is designated by a color, an animal, a bird, a mountain, and other natural phenomena. Tewas associate the north with the color blue, the mountain lion, the oriole, and *Tse Shu P'in* (Hazy or Shimmering Mountain), while the west they associate with the color yellow, the bear, the bluebird, and *Tsikumu P'in* (Obsidian-Covered Mountain). To the south is assigned the color red, the wildcat, the parrot, and *Oekuu P'in* (Turtle Mountain), and to the east belongs white, the wolf, the magpie, and *K'use?P'in* (Stone Man Mountain) (Harrington 1916:41–45; Parsons 1939:365–366; Ortiz 1969:19). Tewas view the directional mountains as sacred because they define the boundaries of the Tewa world. These mountains border an area approximately 140 miles by 35 miles, and each contains a lake or pond and a sacred stone shrine. Each Tewa village also holds sacred certain neighboring hills with additional stone shrines. These nearby features both designate the directions and mark the boundaries of the land immediately surrounding each village.

In Tewa ritual performances, gestures and songs refer to the cardinal directions in the sequence north, west, south, and east. Dancers, singers, and religious leaders may gesture in this sequence during rituals, and dancers often change their facing direction, performing first toward the west, then suddenly pivoting to repeat the movements facing east. Most Tewa dance movements, sequences of movements, or entire dance appearances are repeated four times or in multiples of four, indicating a close connection with the four directions.

When asked about the content of Tewa songs, one composer replied,

> The words we mention in the songs are the directions. We start from the north, we go to the west, south, and east. And when we mention the colors, we start with the blue, yellow, red, and white. And of course we do mention the sacred mountains that are the mountain to the north, the mountain to the west, the mountain to the south, and the one to the east. And then there are some sacred lakes that we have names for there in the north, west, south, and east. And then sometimes we mention the rain clouds, the rain, the thunder, the lightning, the rain gods, and sometimes we mention the rattle we use, and the turtle, and the feathers.

A segment of the San Juan turtle dance song of 1974 illustrates the references to the directions in Tewa songs (Ortiz 1979a):

Away over there, at the dawning place,
Dawn Youths are heard, singing beautifully!
Away over there, at the dawning place,
Dawn Maidens are heard, beautifully making their calls!

Away to the north, holy people are gathering from every direction!
They come, with their corn-growing powers,

And still they come!
Until here they have arrived! (loud rattling)

Away to the west, holy people are gathering from every direction!
They come, with their wheat-growing powers,
And still they come!
Until here they have arrived! (loud rattling)

Away to the south, holy people are gathering from every direction!
They come, with their squash-growing powers, ˌ
And still they come!
Until here they have arrived! (loud rattling)

Away to the east, holy people are gathering from every direction!
They come, with their power to raise all cultigens,
And still they come!
Until here they have arrived! (loud rattling)

The intersection of the four directions marks the center of the Tewa world. Each Tewa Indian, however, also sees his or her village as a center because it is the reference point for the cardinal mountains and lakes (Dozier 1970:209). Within each village, the plazas and kivas are additional centers. How can there be more than one center? In cultural groups like the Tewas, where space is regarded as a most important factor in defining the world, the center is often so significant that it is considered spiritually powerful and sacred. Because of its sacredness, the center of the world can be symbolically represented by several actual places. That is, the center, as sacred space, is forever renewable and can symbolically exist in several places at once (Eliade 1954:20–21; Ortiz 1972:142).

By defining the spatial dimensions of their world through ritual, the Tewas reinforce and strengthen their relationship to the physical environment. Tewa history and culture is intimately connected with the land because unlike many Native American groups, the Tewas managed to remain in the territory settled by their ancestors. Indeed, Tewa cultural survival stems partly from their not having been forced from their ancestral lands. A deep relationship with the land, symbolically stated and restated in ritual, helps the Tewas maintain their distinctive culture.

Time, like space, is perceived differently by different cultural groups. Some think of time as exact measurements along a linear progression. Others, like the Tewas, see time as a never-ending cyclical rhythm connected with solar and lunar movements. This view suggests repeated renewal of life as seasons alternate end-lessly and all forms of life begin, grow, die, and begin once more (Ortiz 1972:137, 143). The dance circuit patterns of village ritual performances reflect this cyclical concept of time. Throughout the day, the dancers and singers per-form in several designated areas, following the same prescribed circuit with each appearance. At times, the entire performance seems to be a continual cycle of repeated movement patterns with only subtle choreographic variations.

The structure of their ritual calendar, in which each event is associated with traditional seasonal tasks, also reflects the Tewas' view of time. The native cal-endar, however, is not the only one that dictates when a village ritual will be held: since contact with Europeans, the Tewa people have also observed certain Catholic holy days. The Catholic and native calendars coexist, with the result that some traditional winter dances are regularly held on or near Christmas and some spring dances are held at Easter. In addition, all the Tewa villages have patron saints who are commemorated by native dances on feast days each year. Santa Clara Tewas, for example, celebrate their feast day every August 12, Saint Clare's Day. Some villages celebrate other saints' days, such as Santiago Day or San Pedro Day, with native dances. Dances performed on Christian holidays communicate both native and Christian meanings and messages. Although the Nambe Tewas may perform the buffalo dance "for the baby Jesus" on December 24 or 25, even dancing in the church itself, the choreography remains un-altered, and native messages about hunting success and need for snow still predominate.

The equinoxes and solstices mark temporal change and solar reversals. They are important times for Tewa ritual performance because they signal seasonal transitions. Village events acknowledge these transitional times, often through symbolic reversals and inversions and through humor. In September, when the growing season is almost over and the hours of sunlight decrease, the clowns become particularly active, publicly displaying behavior that is backwards, improper, and often very funny. Their performances temporarily turn the social world topsy-turvy. Dancers and singers may also take part in symbolic reversals during the equinoxes and solstices. In some events, men impersonate women, and vice versa. Symbolic reversals may include the imitation of outsiders as per-formers dress and act like Anglos, Hispanics, or other Indians, such as Kiowas, Comanches, or Navajos. Just as the natural world is in a state of transition and "confusion" during the equinoxes and solstices, so the Tewa world mirrors it through performance.

In order to better understand Tewa symbolic reversals, as well as Tewa notions of humor, consider the antics of the clowns. Tewa clowns are powerful figures associated with fertility, health, and the sun. As masters of burlesque, they make fun of dancers and singers in solemn public performance, village residents and officials, including the governor, and even the sacred kachinas. Clowns may also tease non-Tewa people, perhaps the local Catholic priest, a nosy anthropologist, or a curious tourist.

In earlier times, Tewa clowns engaged in extraordinarily licentious and destructive behavior. In the twentieth century, clown performances have become much less sexual and violent because of years of pressure from neighboring Hispanics and Anglos and from missionaries who failed to understand that clown behavior reinforces acceptable social norms through negative example. Tewa clown performances, in fact, provide social control by demonstrating how *not* to behave.

Clowns also help integrate foreign institutions, objects, and people into the Tewa world through pantomime and humor. They may poke fun at the Catholic Church by staging a mock Holy Communion during a village ritual performance. After lining up a group of Tewa and non-Tewa observers, they tell each "recipient" to "open your mouth and stick out your tongue." The clowns then give a candy wafer to each puzzled participant. They also play with symbolically loaded objects from outside the Tewa world. A Santa Claus doll might become the object of clown antics around Christmas time, the clown holding and rocking the doll as if it were a real baby. Then suddenly, the clown may lose all interest in the doll, dropping it into the mud.

Clowns especially enjoy singling out and embarrassing Anglo tourists. During a harvest dance at San Ildefonso, a clown convinced a group of Girl Scouts to join the solemn dance line. To the girls' embarrassment, the war captains immediately told them to sit back down. As soon as they did, the clown again convinced them to dance, and again the officers ordered the confused Girl Scouts to leave the dance line. The clown tried a third time, but the girls would not be convinced.

During a midday break in a San Juan performance, a clown insisted that an Anglo woman dance with him in the plaza. He wanted to "disco." After the clown showed off his version of "bumps and grinds," the woman tried gracefully to leave him. The clown would not allow it but instead convinced another clown to perform a mock marriage ceremony for them. Only after they "took their vows" did the clown let his bewildered bride go back to her friends.

San Juan clowns also enjoy borrowing a camera from an Anglo tourist and taking pictures of one another in ludicrous poses. They may also take pictures of the tourist who lent them the camera, thus reversing roles with the outsider and subtly posing the question, "See how it feels to be photographed by a stranger?"

In the Navajo dance, all the Tewa performers engage in symbolic reversals and humorous burlesque. Santa Clara and San Ildefonso present different versions

Figure 19. Through humor and symbolic reversal, the Tewas burlesque the Navajos in their Navajo dance. (Drawing by Rita Newberry, courtesy of Jill D. Sweet.)

of this dance, and the following passage describes it as performed at San Ildefonso in the early spring of 1974 (see Sweet 1979).

The dance was performed by forty women, half of them dressed as Navajo men and half as Navajo women. They wore traditional Navajo clothing, including velveteen shirts and long, full skirts or loose trousers, silver and turquoise jewelry, and Navajo blankets carried over an arm or shoulder. The "women" held ears of corn in their hands and wore their hair tied back with yarn. The "men" wore jeans, Western hats, and boots or moccasins. Many dancers also wore sunglasses, and some of the "men" had fake mustaches or beards (fig. 19).

The performers sang as they danced to the rhythm of a single drum played by a woman also dressed in traditional Navajo fashion. Each "man" shook a rattle throughout the dance. The songs delighted the listeners with English and Navajo phrases such as

I don't care if you've been married sixteen times before,
I'll get you anyway.

I'll treat you better than the one before.
Ya'at'eeh, Ya'at'eeh, I'm a Navajo.

A "campsite," complete with a tent, a tethered horse, and a truck decorated with flowers and the words *Indian Flower Power,* had been set up next to the round kiva. Some women in Navajo garb sat around a campfire, two of them holding Navajo cradleboards containing dolls. During the dance, they handed their "babies" to a Tewa man who rocked them, making the audience laugh.

Throughout the event, dancers held out rugs, blankets, jewelry, and ears of corn to the audience, saying "Hellooo, I haven't seen you in so long, got anything to trade? We're from Ganado" (a Navajo town with a famous trading post). Villagers who were not dancing brought bundles of food and goods to the performers, who carried these gifts of appreciation to the kiva at the end of each dance appearance. During the lunch break, a few Tewa men dressed as Pueblo women took food to the dancers in the kiva, and in the late afternoon there was a throw.

The Navajo dance itself, which included some pantomime, encompassed ten dance appearances of approximately twenty minutes apiece. The dancers began each appearance by singing in Tewa as they walked four abreast from the kiva to the plaza, not in a stylized walk but in a relaxed, comfortable stride. As they walked, the "men" sounded their rattles in accent to the drumbeat. In the plaza, the dancers formed two parallel lines, "women" in one and "men" in the other. The "Navajos" traveled down these lines from west to east, turning inward and pairing up at the end of the line, each couple then traveling back from east to west. Upon reaching the other end of the line, the partners split and repeated the whole sequence. The line formation, however, as well as the steps, gestures, and quality of movement, was completely Tewa, even in parody of the Navajos. During some appearances, a few dancers broke from the line and performed part of the *yeibichai,* a Navajo ritual dance. Even then, they did not abandon the Tewa movement style.

At the fifth appearance, the dancers passed a jug down the line, and each took a gulp; some then staggered backwards as if drunk. Couples occasionally left the line to "waltz" or to have their picture taken by a friend. The Tewa audience laughed uproariously at these antics because they consider such behavior typical of Navajos but improper for themselves.

An understanding of the relationship between Tewas and Navajos is essential to an accurate interpretation of the meanings and messages of the Navajo dance. The two groups have historically been both friends and enemies, and their relationship is one of ambivalence. Intermarriage is not uncommon, and some Tewa families have long-established friendships and trading relationships with Navajo families, whom they regularly visit. Yet, because of cultural differences and a history of conflicts (the Navajos were once seminomadic people who raided Tewa farmers for produce, livestock, and women), some Tewas still regard Navajos as lazy folk who lie, drink, steal, and make poor spouses. Furthermore, the Tewas have always regarded as degrading the Navajo practice of sheep herding.

The Navajo dance permits the Tewas to consider their past and present feelings about Navajos. By mimicking the Navajos, they can ritualize and defuse years of interaction, including some dangerous confrontations. Through humor, the Navajos are symbolically brought into the Tewa world. The Navajo dance also plays up the antithesis of appropriate Tewa behavior, thus reinforcing Tewa standards. Through symbolic reversals and humor, the performance tells Tewa Indians not to drink and act drunk, not to get divorced, and not to be wandering herdsmen.

Besides defining the differences between Tewas and Navajos, the performance plays with male and female role assignment. Tewa women do not normally dress as men (only recently have pants become acceptable attire for Tewa women), nor do men dress as women. Women do not assume important public roles, such as that of drummer, and men do not serve women food in the kiva. The dance temporarily suspends these social rules, and since this suspension is seen as humorous and ridiculous, the norm is reinforced. Village ritual performances such as the Navajo dance, along with clown behavior, illuminate what the Tewas find perplexing, paradoxical, or nonsensical about themselves and others; they use humor to communicate Tewa definitions of proper behavior.

An Annual Cycle

To put into perspective this discussion of Tewa village rituals, it may be helpful to describe, as an example, a typical annual cycle of performances at the village of San Juan. Of all the Tewa villages, San Juan is the largest and is one of the four most ritually active. The other villages historically have regarded San Juan as the "mother village" in ritual and political matters (Ortiz 1969:3).

Each year on January 1, San Juan installs its new secular officers. On January 6, or the closest Sunday thereto, the new officers are honored with a ritual performance. Dancers and singers perform first in the plazas, then in the new officers' homes, where they are given food in gratitude for their performance. The buffalo dance is most often selected for this occasion, probably because at San Juan it involves only a few dancers and the segments can be relatively short.

After the new officers have met with the other council members, the newly composed village council selects a dance to be held in late January or early

February. The choice is usually the basket dance or the cloud dance. By custom, the basket and cloud dances should alternate each year, but this is not always the case. Though both are agricultural dances that once may have been held in early spring, they are now performed in winter because of pressures from early Catholic missionaries who wanted no ritual dancing during Lent.

The night before the performance, male participants hold a short evening dance, a simple line dance offering a prayer for the success of the following day's ritual. A full day of a communal dance such as the basket or cloud dance includes four or more appearances. At San Juan, with each appearance, the group dances first in the south plaza, then in the north plaza, next in the east plaza, and finally in the kiva. Short breaks separate the appearances, and a longer lunch break allows the performers to rest a bit. Often the last circuit is completed just before sunset. Because performances take place on Sunday to accommodate those who work during the week, some families attend mass before the dance begins. While the dance is in progress, women are busy preparing and serving food in their homes. Friends and relatives gather to chat and to share in the feasting.

Unlike the cloud dance, in which only two women at a time dance with the long line of men, the basket dance requires equal numbers of women and men. Before the performance, each man must obtain a pair of notched scraping sticks for his partner; he must either carve them himself or pay another man to make them. Each woman dancer carries these sticks along with a basket, and during part of the dance, she kneels and repeatedly scrapes the sticks over her basket, which functions as a resonator. The result is a beautiful and somewhat eerie droning sound.

San Juan's next ritual performance is selected in January by the unmarried men and boys, who traditionally go to the village game priest and ask if they might hold the deer dance in February. This dance is performed only by men, to songs that are recalled as exactly as possible from previous years. The performance begins with an evening dance, a simple and relatively short prelude in which the dancers ântegeh in place in a single line. At dawn the next morning, the deer dancers dramatically enter the village from hills to the east. They meander slowly as a group of singers chants at the eastern edge of the village.

After the dawn entrance, the deer dancers go to their homes and eat. They return to dance in the plazas repeatedly throughout the day. At the end of the performance, men called "keepers of the deer" shoot rifles and the deer scatter, with San Juan women in pursuit. When a woman catches a dancer, he must give her meat in exchange for stew, bread, cookies, and other cooked foods. As many as a hundred men may participate in the San Juan deer dance.

After the deer dance, the women take a turn at selecting another agricultural dance to be held before Lent. The choice is usually the yellow corn, the spring social, or the butterfly dance, each of which contains agricultural symbols such as corn, squash, or the image of a pollinating insect. They all follow the same basic pattern of appearances and plaza circuits as the basket or the cloud dance. The San Juan butterfly dance, however, features one man and one woman dancer with each appearance, and throughout the day these couples are compared for their dance ability. The choreography of the butterfly dance includes small jumps as the partners move toward or away from each other.

The women may select two of these agricultural dances, and if so, the second is held on Easter Sunday. When they choose only one dance and none is scheduled for Easter, the San Juan people frequently spend the day at another village's ritual performance.

June 13 marks the next regular public event at San Juan: the green corn dance, a celebration for Saint Anthony. In this dance, the singers stand together to one side of the dancers, complementing the words of the songs with gestures that symbolize rain, clouds, and growth.

The one ritual performance that attracts more visitors to San Juan than any other is the patron saint's day celebration on June 24, Saint John's Day (see Sweet 1978). The villagers cannot remember a time when tourists and neighbors did not flock to the event. As early as 1897, a *New York Times* story about the San Juan feast day reported that "200–300 curious Americans" attended. Public activities actually begin on June 23, with vespers in the Catholic church and a buffalo dance in the plazas. The buffalo dancers appear three times, the last at sunset. Though Tewa Indians perform several types of buffalo dances, this version is said to have been borrowed from the Hopis. Its "foreign" origin may explain why it is held in summer at San Juan rather than during the winter, as are most buffalo dances. It may once have been primarily an imitative dance featuring symbolic reversals, one of them being the season of presentation itself. Today, this buffalo dance serves as a prelude to the Comanche dance performed on the following day.

An early morning mass begins the feast day. In recent years, the priest has said much of the mass in Tewa, and sometimes the buffalo dancers perform briefly in the church. After mass, a procession carries the statue of Saint John the Baptist to a cottonwood bower erected in the north plaza. By noon, sixty to one hundred dancers have filed out of the big kiva to perform the Comanche dance. Because this dance is an imitative performance involving a tribal reversal, it seems a logical choice for an event so close to the summer solstice. Still, the dance is not invariably performed every year; in 1983, for example, San Juan presented its green corn dance, which carries no connotations of reversal.

The Comanche dance is one in which Tewa men have considerable freedom in costume construction. They enjoy showing off their most elaborate and garish outfits (fig. 20). It is not uncommon to see male Comanche dancers with dyed feathered war bonnets and bustles, bone breast plates, beaded moccasins, and wild designs of red, blue, yellow, or green face and body paint. Most elements of a male Comanche costume are traded for or purchased from Plains Indians at intertribal gatherings called powwows. Unlike their male counterparts, Tewa women who perform in the Comanche dance are conservatively attired in typical Pueblo dresses, with a lace-trimmed shawl over one shoulder and a woven sash at the waist. The difference in costume is echoed in the execution of the dance steps; the men exaggerate Tewa movements and frequently let out loud yelps, whereas the women remain demure and perform their movements as they would for any other Tewa dance.

All day the village is crowded with Anglos, Hispanics, Tewas, and other Indian visitors. When the dancing and feasting are over, a small group of San Juan Indians, Hispanics, and the Catholic priest return the statue of Saint John to the church. The Hispanic participants are neighbors who often join in the activities of the San Juan church.

San Juan consultants say that this event is "to honor the saint," but the performance also celebrates the power of the sun at the summer solstice and symbolically helps the sun change its path. Early descriptions of this celebration mention not only song and dance but also ritual foot races (Jackson 1882:106–107). At San Juan, this traditionally was a relay race between two teams, one made up of men from the north side of the village and the other of men from the south side. The race track ran from east to west, like the path of the sun (Ortiz 1969:108–110). San Juan's patron saints' day celebration clearly has both Catholic and traditional Tewa religious foundations.

Another important part of the feast day is the carnival that is set up at the edge of the village, spatially separated from the plaza dancing. Run by several Hispanic and Anglo families who travel to many summer feast day celebrations around the state, the carnival is one of the day's highlights for the San Juan children. Some tourists complain that the carnival "spoils" the authenticity of the Indian event, but Tewas say that the carnival has been part of the celebration for as long as they can remember.

The next public performance at San Juan, though not held every year, is the harvest dance sponsored by the kossa clown society in mid September. One San Juan man explained that its purpose is "to feed Mother Nature for the crops that have been provided you for the year." In the harvest dance, an entrance song and dance sequence is followed by nine more sequences, with no breaks between songs, not even a lunch rest. Each sequence is dedicated to a specific ceremonial society or other social group within the community. The dancers form a circle, and as each social group is mentioned in the song, its members identify themselves by moving out from the circle. In this way, the dance publicly defines each dancer's place in the San Juan social system. An impressive throw accompanies the harvest dance as hundreds of items are tossed to the singers, dancers, and observers.

The Christmas *matachines* dance is the next public performance held in San Juan (fig. 21). Of Spanish derivation, the dance has a European Christian theme; the San Juan Indians say that it was "taught to us long ago by the missionaries." Perhaps because of its foreign origin, the village governor and staff are responsible for organizing the performance.

Some researchers argue that the matachines dance symbolizes the battles between Christians and Moors, while others claim that it depicts the legend of Montezuma (see Lyon 1979; Champe 1983). Its European origin, however, is not debated. The music has been traced to sixteenth-century European tunes, and the Tewas often hire Hispanic musicians to play the violin and guitar for the event. Matachines dance steps feature skips, turns, and other movements not typical of Tewa dance. One Tewa man observed that the matachines dance could not be Tewa in origin because the steps begin on the left foot and Tewa steps always begin on the right foot.

After the matachines dance on December 25, there is a sunset dance or prelude to the turtle dance, which is performed the following day. The San Juan Indians consider the turtle dance to be their most important public ritual. It is not a Christmas celebration but a winter solstice ritual marking the end of one and the beginning of another annual cycle.

For several evenings before the turtle dance, two *tsave yoh* visit San Juan. The village war captains impersonate these beings, who live in caves in the four sacred hills. The white-masked tsave yoh, associated with the winter moiety, enters the village from the north, while the black-masked tsave yoh, associated with the summer moiety, enters from the south. Both carry whips and flog any San Juan residents who have behaved particularly poorly during the year. Although the whipping is more a symbolic gesture than a serious assault, most villagers avoid getting too close to the tsave yoh. Despite their masks, these figures are not kachinas.

On the day of the turtle dance, the tsave yoh police the village, whipping any troublemakers. Tourists are not spared. The clowns also appear in San Juan for the turtle dance, which choreographically is one of the simplest. The single line of male dancers never changes formation as the men ântegeh in place, occasionally pivoting to face a different direction. The dancers are supposed to sing clearly, with no drum or chorus to accompany them.

The dances in the cycle just described do not exhaust the list, but they do include those most regularly performed. Other Tewa villages perform some of

Figure 20. A young Comanche dancer at San Juan shows off a gaudy costume and elaborate face paint. (Photo by Roger Sweet, 1974.)

Figure 21. San Juan matachines dancers wear miters with long, colorful ribbons hanging down the back and cover their faces with black fringe and scarves. (Photo by Roger Sweet, 1974.)

the same dances, in addition to ones that are not part of the San Juan ritual cycle. San Juan consultants say that some dances have fallen from their repertoire while others have been consciously revived. Most recent among the revivals is the spring social dance, which in 1972 was performed for the first time in more than twenty years. In 1964, San Juan revived its green corn dance, and in 1951, the yellow corn dance. These revivals occur when individuals in the village become concerned about cultural continuity and encourage the elders to work with village song composers to recall songs and dances that have not been performed for many years.

About the revival efforts, one San Juan man said, "We're trying to get our customs up again instead of them being buried." Another noted, "Within the past few years, more of the younger generation are taking part in it [dance events]—which is good—because we're trying to emphasize to the school kids that this is their doings, their culture, and we want to keep it going." A third San Juan man happily acknowledged the resurgence in dance participation, saying, "The dance lines keep getting longer and younger."

Figure 22. San Ildefonso Pueblo Comanche dancers in Plains Indian headdresses. (Photo by Roger Sweet, 1973)

CHAPTER THREE

THEATRICAL PRODUCTIONS

Anglo travelers from the East became fascinated with Tewa village ritual performances as early as the 1890s (see Eickemeyer and Eickemeyer 1895). Traveling for pleasure was rare, however, until the completion of the railroads in the early 1900s, when the number of visitors increased dramatically. A small group of Anglo businessmen saw tourism as a way to achieve economic growth and even statehood for the territory of New Mexico. They began to advertise in eastern magazines and newspapers the Southwest's healthful climate, beautiful landscapes, prehistoric ruins, and fascinating and peaceful Indians.

By the 1920s, tourists could visit a Tewa village as part of a packaged "Indian Detour" sponsored by the Santa Fe Railroad and the Fred Harvey Company, a hotel and restaurant developer rapidly expanding in the Southwest (see Thomas 1978). The Tewa villages most often toured were Tesuque, Santa Clara, San Ildefonso, and San Juan. If a village ritual was not in progress, the tour guide might ask a few Tewa Indians to perform a short dance segment, and the tourists would drop coins onto a drum for the dancers.

While the Indian Detours were taking tourists out to the Pueblo villages, some Southwestern businessmen decided that bringing the Indians to the tourists might be more profitable. They established annual theatrical productions called *ceremonials* in major New Mexico towns, events that became important tourist attractions in the Southwest. Through these events, the Tewas began to export segments of their dances and songs. Dancing in a ceremonial, Tewas found themselves in a performance situation very different from that of the traditional village events, one primarily theatrical rather than ritual. Today, many

Tewa Indians move comfortably from village rituals to commercial theatrical productions, but they have carefully maintained their village performances as separate, and far more important, events.

Anglo-Organized Ceremonials

Ceremonials were the first elaborate theatrical productions to focus on Southwestern Indian performance. Advertised as tributes to the American Indian, they were nonetheless designed primarily to promote tourism. For a brief time, Gallup, Albuquerque, and Santa Fe each tried to make its ceremonial the most spectacular. The Albuquerque ceremonial was short-lived, and the Santa Fe event soon became an arts and crafts fair. Gallup holds the only remaining Anglo-organized annual ceremonial, and it still attracts thousands of visitors.

The first Gallup Inter-Tribal Indian Ceremonial was organized by Mike Kirk, owner of a local trading post. It was held in September of 1922 and brought to the town more than two thousand Indian participants and observers. Besides dancing, the early Gallup ceremonials included Navajo sandpainting demonstrations, parades, baseball games, foot races, horse races, rodeo events, and arts and crafts exhibits (fig. 23). The organizers of the 1925 Gallup ceremonial even imported buffalo to stampede through the grounds every afternoon. (The animals caused considerable property damage.) Also part of the early Gallup ceremonials was a "chicken pull," an event later dropped because animal protection societies protested it as inhumane. This "sport" was probably introduced by the early Spaniards, and chicken pulls are still held at many Pueblo villages on San Pedro Day and Santiago Day.

The economic impact of the ceremonials on the town of Gallup is difficult to determine. In a dissertation on this subject, Terry Carroll (1971:69) found that the early economic advantages could not be documented, even after an exhaustive search of the ceremonial association's records. The records indicate only idealistic motives for the ceremonial. For example, the printed program for the 1924 ceremonial expressed humanitarian reasons for the event:

> It was thought by the people of [Gallup] that due to the advantageous location, that something should be done to create good feelings among the various tribes and to stimulate their interest in weaving better blankets, making better pottery and growing better crops. This idea had the cooperation of the Indian Department, and the agents of the various tribes and divisions of tribes.

In spite of the unselfish claims of Anglo organizers, some Indians have seen the event in less than positive terms. In the earliest years, Mike Kirk reportedly spent long days in Pueblo councils trying to convince elders to allow their young

Figure 23. A poster advertising the 1941 Gallup Inter-Tribal Indian Ceremonial. (School of American Research collections; photo by Deborah Flynn.)

people to take part in the Gallup ceremonials (Huff 1946:58). Much later, Indian participants loudly expressed dissatisfaction during a 1954 meeting of Pueblo groups to discuss issues of better pay, protection of civil rights in Gallup, and insurance for Indian performers. The Pueblo Indians threatened to boycott the ceremonial if their demands were not met (Carroll 1971:167–168). The boycott proved unnecessary, however, and they succeeded in getting a pay raise from seventeen to twenty dollars for participating in all performances. The Indians demonstrated that they could hurt Gallup's tourist business; attendance at the ceremonial that year dropped by two thousand people, apparently the result of publicity about their complaints.

The Gallup ceremonials also generated problems between the Anglo organizers and the Indian participants because they were based heavily on competition. Contests in sports, arts and crafts, and dances were most often judged only by Anglos, whose values differed from those of the Indian performers. Not understanding the Tewa language, Anglo judges paid little or no attention to song composition. The Tewa people, on the other hand, consider the song an integral part of a dance performance. Anglo judges also looked for energetic dancers with "spirit" or "pep." According to Tewa standards, however, it is a poor dancer who stands out by "dancing too hard." In the late 1970s, the Gallup dance competitions were eliminated, although performances continued.

In spite of the objections expressed by Anglos and Indians over the years, many Indians still look forward to the Gallup ceremonial as an opportunity to see old friends and have a good time. Participants come from all over the country and even from Mexico and Canada.

Apparently, the Tewas first participated in a Gallup ceremonial in 1923, when Tesuque dancers were contracted to perform short segments of the bow and arrow, buffalo, and eagle dances and a San Juan group performed segments of the buffalo, basket, war, deer, dog, turtle, and butterfly dances. Of all the Tewa villages, San Juan continues to appear most regularly in the Gallup ceremonials.

Today, the Gallup ceremonial begins with a parade of marching bands, floats, antique cars, wagons, and horses. A ceremonial Indian queen and princesses ride in the parade, and the American and New Mexican flags are prominently displayed. During the four days of the ceremonial, currently held at Red Rock State Park, many activities take place simultaneously. Indian children perform short dance segments in the two small dance plazas while a rodeo goes on in an arena nearby. Exhibits of Native American arts and crafts include frequent demonstrations of rug weaving, sand painting, woodcarving, jewelry making, and potting. Throughout the park, vendors set up booths to sell Indian food.

Each day culminates in an evening dance performance. The show begins with an Indian blessing, followed by a fire lighting ceremony, the singing of the Star

Spangled Banner, and a grand entrance of all the costumed performers. For the rest of the evening, dance groups perform in turn, each for twenty minutes or less. The show concludes as all the participants circle and exit in procession. The dancers earn twenty dollars per performance.

Six years after the first Gallup ceremonial, Albuquerque staged a ceremonial called "The First American." Mike Kirk also organized this event and made it spectacular indeed. He ordered ten thousand programs, a color lighting system, and twenty Indian tepees. He contracted six hundred Indians from Mexico, Colorado, Oklahoma, Washington, Arizona, and New Mexico, and to climax the event, eighteen tribes performed different dances simultaneously. A September 13, 1928, article in the *Albuquerque Journal* described the finale: "After a few minutes of this big dance, the dancers weave out of the picture, leaving on the very topmost point [of an adobe structure] a lone Indian, bow in hand, arrow shaft drawn to the head—the symbolic figure of the last arrow."

There was great support for The First American. A local radio station broadcast the event, and Paramount Pictures filmed the grand finale. But ticket sales did not cover expenses. Although considered a theatrical success, the ceremonial suffered losses so great that it was held only for a few more years and never again as lavishly.

Santa Fe's annual event honoring the Indian and promoting tourism began as part of the 1919 revival of the Santa Fe Fiesta. The revival was shaped largely by Edgar Hewett, an energetic anthropologist who directed the School of American Research and the Museum of New Mexico. Hewett, genuinely concerned for the survival of Indian culture, was not directly interested in tourist dollars, but he received much financial support for the event from local merchants primarily interested in tourism.

For the first three years of the revived fiesta, one day of three was devoted to Indian culture. In 1922, this Indian day became a three-day Indian market held at a separate location. About forty years later, the Indian market split completely from the fiesta and was even assigned a different weekend.

The Santa Fe Indian Market does not focus on performance; it is an arts and crafts fair rather than a ceremonial. Indian vendors display and sell their arts, crafts, and foods from tables and booths that fill the town's plaza. The Southwestern Association on Indian Affairs (SWAIA) contracts dancers to perform short segments in the patio of the Palace of the Governors. Again, they receive twenty dollars per performance. An Indian master of ceremonies provides tourists with some background information about Pueblo life and beliefs, then gives a brief explanation before each dance segment. Each group performs twice during the afternoon, and at the end of the day, Indian judges announce the prize-winning groups. The Santa Fe Indian Market attracts thousands of visitors each year.

Tewa-Organized Ceremonials

Although Tewas participated in Anglo-organized ceremonials, Indians never had a strong voice in their organization. With the establishment of the first Tewa-organized ceremonial in 1957, the situation changed.

The first such ceremonial, sponsored and organized by the Santa Clara Tewas, was held at Puye Cliffs, a prehistoric site ten miles west of the village (fig. 24). The Santa Claras believe that their ancestors once lived there. Archaeologists may argue this point, but their debates do not trouble most Santa Clara people, who consider the two-mile stretch of cliff dwellings as part of their heritage (Arnon and Hill 1979:269).

Juan Chavarria, a leader in the Santa Clara community, originally proposed the Puye Cliffs event. As a boy, he imagined a day when his people might dance among the ancient pueblo ruins:

> When I was a boy, going through here [Puye Cliffs area], my dad and I used to go for wood back here in a wagon—pass by here sitting there in the wagon and looking this way towards the cliffs—and in my own mind—or dream away somewhere beyond—I'd say, "It would be wonderful if the people from Santa Clara could come up here for one day, or two days, and perform right in the very plaza that our ancestors performed these very dances." And so that was on my mind all that time. And for a few years, I was out of the pueblo and even at that time, when I was in Denver, I used to think about it, "Well, when I go back, I'll see what I can do about it."

After living in Denver, Chavarria returned to Santa Clara and was elected governor of the village. During his third term, he suggested to the village council that Santa Clara sponsor a ceremonial at the cliffs site. At first, some council members opposed the idea because they feared that tourists would disrupt the area. But Chavarria convinced his colleagues, and the first Puye Cliffs ceremonial was held in August of 1957. It continued as an annual event until 1982.

For the first three years of the Puye Cliffs ceremonial, only Santa Clara Indians participated. In 1961, organizers invited the Jicarilla Apaches and Tesuque, Nambe, and Taos pueblos to send dancers. In later years, San Ildefonso and San Juan also took part. The majority of the dance segments, however, were performed by Santa Clara dancers.

As with the Anglo-organized ceremonials, the Puye Cliffs celebration was not always profitable. Although the organizing committee worked without pay, costs of advertising the two-day event and payroll for the dancers sometimes exceeded proceeds. According to Chavarria, when there was a profit, it usually

Figure 24. A poster promoting the Puye Cliffs ceremonial for 1961. (School of American Research collections; photo by Deborah Flynn.)

went towards the following year's expenses. The people who most directly bene-fited from the Puye ceremonials were the food vendors and those who sold arts and crafts. The dancers earned twenty-five dollars per day for their participation.

A Santa Clara elder usually opened the Puye Cliffs ceremonials with an invo-cation in Tewa, generally a prayer for peaceful and healthful living. The Pueblo governor then gave a welcoming speech in English and reminded the audience that "everything done here should be taken seriously." Following the governor's speech, Mr. Chavarria briefed the audience on the history of the Puye Cliffs ceremonials and outlined some basic beliefs and traditions of the Tewas. He usu-ally noted the significance of the area as the home of the Santa Claras' ancestors: "We're dancing today to the Great Spirit for rain, crops, and to honor our ances-tors that lived a contented and unhurried life here."

After the introductory speeches, the short dance segments began. Each dance group prepared for its performance in the partially restored rooms northeast of the dance plaza, briefly practicing there before going in front of the audience. As the dancers walked toward the dance area, they often sprinkled sacred cornmeal on the ground.

Segments of more than twenty different Tewa dances have been performed at Puye. Each dance segment contained two, three, or four repeated movement sequences, each performed facing a new direction. After the plaza performance, some groups repeated a short section on returning to the dressing room. Sometimes, at the end of the day, a round dance was performed, with the audience invited to join.

Santa Clara Tewas are quick to point out that they tried to minimize the non-Indian aspects of their ceremonials. There were no competitions or awards, no sports events, no marching bands or parades, and no queen contests. Replacing the American flag was a banner of Pueblo design.

Juan Chavarria took the Puye Cliffs ceremonials seriously. He believed that the dancing united Santa Claras with their past and promoted cultural pride among the young people. He also held that the dancers participated with the same dedication required for a village ritual:

> I know for sure that [the ancestors] are out there in spirit among the dancers…and I very much believe that they are among us and that we are all taking part in dancing—as well as when we are dancing in the pueblo—the same feeling—you have to put your whole heart and yourself into what dances you are taking part in—no matter where you are dancing.

The Puye Cliffs ceremonial has not been held since 1981, when the show ended tragically as lightning struck and killed two Indian women. Some of the

Tewa people interpreted the incident as a supernatural warning that the event should no longer be held, and the Santa Clara village council announced the decision to discontinue it in 1982.

The second Tewa-organized ceremonial, the Nambe Falls event, was established four years after the first Puye Cliffs ceremonial. It has been held every year since 1961, except for 1982, when "the people just didn't get it organized," perhaps reflecting some hesitation because of the Puye Cliffs incident.

A group of concerned Nambe residents began planning the first Nambe ceremonial when the deteriorating village church was declared unsafe in the late 1950s. The Nambe people had to raise funds to replace the condemned building, and their St. Francis Women's Club offered a solution. The club formed a committee to organize an annual ceremonial, all proceeds of which were to be set aside for the new church. Since the primary purpose for holding the event was to raise money for the church, the committee selected a July 4 performance date because it was likely to draw large crowds (fig. 25).

The first Nambe ceremonial was held in 1961 in the village itself, after which the organizers moved its location to the Nambe Falls area, four miles to the west. Just as the Santa Clara Tewas hold Puye Cliffs important, Nambe Indians say that the falls area has always been sacred to them. Near the falls are natural rock formations resembling two large serpents (some people claim that there is only one) to which have been ascribed supernatural powers. An early anthropologist who worked with the Nambe Indians, Elsie Clews Parsons, recorded stories about a serpent that had the power to flood the village (Parsons 1929:275).

While the community was raising money for the new church, all revenue from the Nambe Falls ceremonials went to the building fund, and responsibility for organizing the event was shared by the women's church committee and the village governor. With the completion of the church, only part of the revenue was needed for its maintenance, and the rest was available for other community projects. With this change, organizational responsibilities moved from the church committee to the village officials. Since the ceremonial was established as a fund-raising event, Nambe dancers have never been paid to participate, and the cost of producing the Nambe Falls ceremonial is minimal.

Unlike the Puye Cliffs ceremonials, the Nambe Falls event generally begins with a flag-raising ceremony. Several costumed dancers hoist up the United States and New Mexico flags, along with a Nambe village flag, to the accompaniment of the national anthem. Next, an invocation in Tewa is usually offered by Moses Peña, an elderly Nambe man whom many residents affectionately call "Uncle Moses." After the tribal governor's welcoming speech, the dancing and singing begin. Nambe people perform most of the dance segments, but San Ildefonso, San Juan, and Santa Clara dancers sometimes perform as well. The event

Figure 25 Buffalo dancers at a Nambe Falls ceremonial draw a large audience. (Photo by Roger Sweet, 1973.)

generally closes with another prayer in Tewa by Moses Peña, and in some years the community gathers in a round dance after most of the visitors have left.

Although the Nambe Falls ceremonial began in support of the Catholic church in Nambe, the event has served to renew interest in traditional ritual performances. Nambe people say that the event gives their children an extra chance to learn traditional dances, an opportunity that is particularly important for the Nambe community because it has suffered greater cultural disruption than some of the other Tewa villages. By the mid-twentieth century, all of Nambe's native religious leaders had died unable to pass their ritual training on to the younger generation because many young people were uninterested or were away at school. The establishment of the falls event has helped significantly in revitalization.

Nambe residents speak of the falls ceremonial as a time for cooperating in a community effort, seeing old friends, and having fun. They also describe it as an event that promotes long life and health, just as a village ritual does. When asked to consider differences between dancing in the village and dancing at the falls, some said that in village rituals the dance must be repeated at least four times but at the falls this is not necessary. Dances performed at the falls need not be consistent with a proper season; winter animal dances could be performed as frequently as agricultural dances in spite of the July date. In addition, one Nambe man pointed out that at the falls he dances with a little "more action for show" than in the village. These three differences are found in Tewa performances during other types of theatrical productions as well.

Other Theatrical Performances

Despite the survival of only two ceremonials—Gallup and Nambe Falls—theatrical performances of Tewa dances can still be seen at many events, both Tewa- and Anglo-organized. Among the events that seem to be growing in popularity are the Southwestern arts and crafts fairs, in which dancing and singing are simply background entertainment that helps create an authentic ethnic atmosphere for the main business of selling art work. Arts and crafts fairs have greater economic potential than do ceremonials because they give the Tewas and other Indians a chance to sell their goods without middleman costs.

The most important fair for the Tewas is the Eight Northern Indian Pueblo Council (ENIPC) Artist and Craftsman Show, the first Indian-owned-and-operated art show. This two-day fair has been held every July since 1973 at one of the eight northern Pueblo villages (the six Tewa villages, Picuris, and Taos), annually attracting more than three hundred craftsmen and ten thousand to twelve thousand visitors. Cash prizes donated by local organizations and businesses are awarded for the arts and crafts. Regulations ensure the quality and authenticity of the products shown, and participation is limited to Native Americans, some of whom travel from as far away as Canada.

The ENIPC Artist and Craftsman Show includes short segments of Pueblo dancing in a roped-off area to one side of the sales booths (fig. 26). Usually, this is not the same part of the village where the traditional ritual dances are held, nor are the kivas used for performer preparation. In most respects, performances at the ENIPC fair resemble those at Tewa-organized ceremonials, but Pueblo Indian judges have always given cash awards for the "best" dances. This practice is clearly an Anglo one adopted from the earliest ceremonials. As at the Puye Cliffs event, performers are paid twenty dollars per day.

Ceremonials and arts and crafts fairs are not the only theatrical events in which the Tewas perform. Since the early 1900s, Tewa dancers and singers have appeared in varied and far-flung events, most of them Anglo-organized. In 1915, for example, Edgar Hewett, mastermind of the early Santa Fe Fiestas, invited a group of San Ildefonso Tewas to dance at the New Mexico state exhibit for the Panama-California Exposition in San Diego. In subsequent years, Hewett's School of American Research in Santa Fe sponsored performances in which Tewa and other Pueblo Indians demonstrated their dances and songs in an auditorium, primarily for New Mexican audiences.

Figure 26. A group of San Juan Tewas presents a segment of the basket dance during the ENIPC Artist and Craftsman Show. (Photo by Roger Sweet, 1974.)

Another early organizer of Pueblo performances outside New Mexico was John Collier, a social reformer and defender of Indian rights who later became U.S. commissioner of Indian affairs. Collier's purpose was primarily political: by bringing delegations of Tewa and other Pueblo dancers and singers to the East, he attempted to raise money and gain votes for or against specific bills that would affect the Indians (Philip 1977:55–70). During the 1920s, he arranged performances in Washington, D.C., and even took a group to perform in the New York Stock Exchange, hoping to convince wealthy businessmen to write letters in support of Indian rights.

Today, Tewas continue to perform occasionally for political purposes, sometimes dancing and singing at the state capitol in Santa Fe to influence legislators on issues that would affect the lives of the Pueblo people. They also travel to various cultural festivals and fairs. Several Canadian Mariposa festivals during the late 1970s and early 1980s featured Tewa presentations, as did the Smithsonian Native American Folk Festival of 1976. In 1979, the Smithsonian again invited the Tewas to dance in Washington, D.C., this time in honor of Pope John Paul II. Shortly before mass was celebrated, the Tewas presented a buffalo dance for the pope and a crowd estimated at 175,000 people.

Like other Native Americans from all over the United States and Canada, Tewas sometimes attend intertribal powwows, which are Indian-organized gatherings held in all major American cities and many western rural areas. They are primarily social events featuring Indian dancing and singing, and Tewa groups may be among those invited to perform.

Closer to home, the Tewas dance every September at the New Mexico State Fair in Albuquerque, in a section of the fairgrounds designated as Indian Village. They perform for local elementary and high schools; the San Juan bilingual elementary schools even invited an elder dance group leader to teach the children Tewa songs and dances. Universities in New Mexico, California, and Utah have also hosted Tewa dancers and singers.

Visitors to New Mexico can see Tewas perform at the Indian Pueblo Cultural Center in Albuquerque. Run by the All-Indian Pueblo Council, a group of leaders from twenty Pueblo villages, it features an art museum, a gift shop, and a restaurant, all displaying and selling Indian products. Each weekend throughout the summer, the Indian Pueblo Cultural Center sponsors dance and song performances by various Pueblo groups.

Ritual and Theater

Ritual and theater communicate emotions, ideas, and images, making statements about the nature of humans and their environment, about life and death, good and evil, and other concepts central to a people's worldview. Though ritual and theater often overlap, with "elements of theatre in ritual and… elements of ritual in theatre" (Schechner 1977:78), they can be distinguished because each has a different primary purpose.

Most rituals are intended to bring people closer to the supernatural world and to aid in transforming phases in seasonal or life cycles. Their ultimate goal is to restore some order and balance among the social, natural, and supernatural worlds. Because rituals are believed to be essential for the group's survival, participation can be an indispensable obligation to the community. Theater events, in contrast, are held primarily for entertainment. Participation is more a matter of choice than of necessity, motivated by economic gain and the performers' desire for creative expression and professional recognition. The goal of theater is to please the audience on which it depends for financial success.

Tewa village performances, of course, represent the ritual end of the ritual-theater continuum. They are regarded by the people as vital expressions of unity, necessary for cultural survival. Performances at Anglo-organized ceremonials and other events lie near the theater end of the continuum. Somewhere in the middle, sharing elements of both, fall the dance performances at ceremonials and other shows organized by the Tewas themselves (see Sweet 1983).

Several scholars have distinguished ritual from theater partly by the nature of their audiences (Rappaport 1979:177; Schechner 1977:79; Leach 1976:45). A ritual audience is participatory; audience and performer may even be one and the same. Supernaturals can also be present. The ritual audience accepts and often believes the symbolic presentation, requiring no written or spoken aids to understanding. A theater audience, on the other hand, merely watches, sitting in judgment without actively participating. Theater audiences often expect a written or verbal explanation of the performance, so programs are provided as guides for understanding the presentation and identifying individual performers.

Tewa audiences at village rituals consider their role to be one of active listening, and they contribute their thoughts to the community prayer that is being offered. In contrast, audiences at Anglo-organized ceremonials and other theatrical performances seldom understand the Tewa songs or the meanings of costumes and gestures and need explanations to help them appreciate the performance. Program notes and masters of ceremonies—today, usually Indians—keep their explanations of cultural concepts expediently brief, providing only key phrases and words, such as "harmony with the natural or supernatural worlds," "weather control," "rain," "corn," "success in hunting," "love for tribal lands," "Mother Earth," and "Great Spirit." These expressions serve as a kind of shorthand alluding to much deeper concepts.

Audience participation in theater is ordinarily limited to the conventional expression of approval by applause. Although this custom is not practiced during ritual performance, Tewa dancers have adjusted to it at theatrical productions and have even come to expect it. They say that enthusiastic applause makes them feel proud. Even the Tewas in a theatrical-production audience applaud the performers.

The Tewa audience rarely leaves a ritual because of snow or rain; the dancers do not run for shelter or cancel the performance. Precipitation during a village dance is, after all, a blessing and often the very purpose of the event. Ceremonial audiences, on the other hand, quickly leave if there is a summer shower, and they expect the show to stop. Dance contracts even have clauses stating that the performance will be cancelled if the weather proves uncooperative and only partial payment will be made to the dancers.

Competition is another area of difference. In village performance, it is not totally foreign to Tewa tradition but is treated with great subtlety. In the butterfly dance, for example, the dance style of each couple is compared to that of the others, but those judged most skillful are given little public recognition. Emphasis on the entire group takes precedence over competitive aspects.

As mentioned earlier, the Anglo organizers of ceremonials stressed competition in all activities. They offered prizes for outstanding dances, arts and crafts, and sports, clearly using competition to keep the shows exciting. Their rationale—that competition would promote better quality and more authentic products and performances by Indians—seems in retrospect paternalistic.

The contractual relationship between organizer and performer also differentiates the theatrical from the ritual. Anglo organizers pay cash for contracted performances, whereas in village events the dancers are given food and other gifts for their participation. When a relative pins money on a dancer's costume, the act simply reflects the communal reciprocity system.

Anglo ceremonial contracts limit the number of dancers who can participate in a show; organizers tell dance group leaders how many dancers will be paid. If more dancers perform, the share of each is diminished, so it is desirable to keep the dance group small. Limiting the size of the dance group contrasts with traditional values, which hold that the more participants there are, the more powerful the event will be. In some cases, performance contracts led to exclusiveness because the dance group leader could select the same few family members year after year, sometimes drawing resentment from other members of the community.

Anglo ceremonial organizers quickly learned that their audiences expected a concise show with a constant flow of varied entertainment. They found that many short segments were more entertaining than a few long dances, and they contractually limited the length of a performance to one dance segment of ten or twenty minutes. A complete performance of this length was another new concept for the Tewa Indians, whose rituals can be all-day events.

Tewas usually restrict photography and sound recording during village rituals, whereas the ceremonial performance contract stipulates permission to be photographed or recorded. Along with Anglo tourists, some Tewas now have pictures of the dances and tapes of the songs that they can enjoy at home.

Adherence to clock and calendar is another feature distinguishing Anglo-organized performances from Tewa village rituals. Village performances are keyed to the seasons, and except for those that have become linked to Christian holidays, they are held on no fixed date. Neither do they begin at any fixed time, but only when the participants are ready and all necessary preparations are complete. Anglo-organized events, on the other hand, are usually scheduled for July or August, at the height of the tourist season. They generally run by the clock, their schedules rigidly adhered to so that the audience is not inconvenienced. Dance groups who arrive late upset both audience and organizers and are not invited back.

A final contrast lies in the concept of place. Tewas hold their village rituals in plazas and kivas, areas that symbolize the heart of the Tewa world. Anglo-organized performances require instead an accessible location large enough to accommodate many people. They are often held in places designed to provide comfort for the audience and to keep performers and audience separated.

The practice of "finishing a dance," a custom that began during the 1920s when the Tewas first performed at Anglo-organized ceremonials, demonstrates the importance of sacred village space. To finish a dance, performers who had danced in a ceremonial repeated their presentation in the village plaza upon their return. The practice was an extension of a Tewa metaphor in which a ritual performance is "like a plant":

> When the date for the ceremony is set, it is believed that a crack appears in the earth where the seed of the dance has sprouted. The song composing and practice sessions in preparation for the dance are viewed as being analogous to the stage of growth of the plant. The day of the dance itself is considered the day when the plant bears fruit. (Ortiz 1977:18)

As long as a dance was planned, rehearsed, and finally repeated or finished in the village, it could be said to have "sprouted," "grown," and "born fruit" at home, just as it did during a traditional village ritual. It became irrelevant that the dance was taken away to a theatrical show between stages of growth. Tewa consultants say that finishing a dance brought the songs and movements back to the village, expressed gratitude for a safe journey, and showed the rest of the community how well a group performed for its non-Tewa audience. The custom also ensured that the meanings and prayers of the performance still reached the village.

Finishing a dance was an effort to legitimize a theatrical performance. It helped to reduce fears that exporting the dances and songs might undermine the village rituals. The practice was reported for the Nambe Tewas of the 1920s (Parsons 1929:n.345) and the Santa Claras of the 1930s (Gilbert 1940:43). San Juan performers still finished dances occasionally during the 1970s. Today, however, the practice has nearly died out. A woman from San Juan said that all dances and songs performed outside the village should be finished at home, but "it is not done as often as in the old days—I guess because some of them, they get lazy about it." Perhaps dances are no longer finished regularly because the Tewas now feel more confident that exporting dances will not weaken their village rituals. Their concerns may continue to diminish as they become increasingly familiar with and comfortable in places outside their traditional world. It is noteworthy that during the 1970s, the likelihood of a dance being finished at San Juan increased with the distance traveled by the performers. Dances performed out of the state or country were more often finished in the village than those performed in Albuquerque or Santa Fe.

Although village events are primarily ritual and Anglo-organized events primarily theater, Tewa-organized theatrical performances are hybrids of both. The Anglo-organized ceremonials stimulated many innovations: a financial motive; the acceptance of a largely non-Indian audience and of applause; the scheduling of a variety of short dance segments rather than one long, repetitive ritual performance; and the presentation of an explanatory speech before the performance. Tewa organizers also recognized the economic wisdom of holding theatrical events during the summer tourist season.

Yet, ritual elements remain strong features of Tewa-organized theatrical performances. Competition is often absent, and even some of those Tewas who favor dance competitions at Anglo-organized events feel that they are inappropriate for Tewa-organized performances. Formal dance contracts are not used, nor is dance group size limited. Dancers from other villages may arrive unexpectedly, and often it is not certain exactly who will perform until minutes before the show begins. At least in the case of Tewa-organized ceremonials, the choice of place is not dictated by convenience to the tourist but by the ritual importance the site holds for the Tewas. Finally, the content of the Tewa-organized performances is close to that of their village rituals, centering on song and dance and avoiding parades, rodeos, and queen contests.

Anglo-organized ceremonials, Tewa-organized ceremonials, and performances at arts and crafts fairs and other events all enable visitors to see some aspects of Tewa Indian culture. Though different from village ritual performances, these theatrical productions are Southwestern traditions. They can give visitors an opportunity to experience as many as seven or eight different dances in one afternoon and to compare performances of the same dance by groups from several different Tewa villages. Variations in dance style, choreography, songs, and costumes can be observed, an advantage for travelers who are short on time. All the theatrical productions are lively and colorful events that both Tewas and visitors can enjoy.

Figure 27. Crowds of visitors gather to watch and photograph the butterfly dance during a Puye Cliffs ceremonial. (Photo by Roger Sweet, 1973.)

CHAPTER FOUR
VISITORS
IN THE TEWA WORLD

Tourists and other outsiders have converged on Tewa ritual performances for so many years that the Tewas have come to expect them as audience members. At theatrical performances, visitors are even an integral part of the event (fig. 27). These visitors include individuals or groups traveling for pleasure (most often Anglos), as well as local Hispanic, Anglo, Pueblo, and non-Pueblo Indian neighbors. Only rarely, during the colder months, are outsiders few or absent.

The most numerous visitors are the Anglo tourists who come to Tewa villages seeking an exotic cultural experience or a glimpse of what seems to be the simpler, less fragmented existence of a traditional culture. Typically, these visitors see Tewa villages as relatively uncomplicated and unified communities where ritual is part of the people's lives and the group exists harmoniously with nature.

To some Tewa Indians, conversely, tourists seem suspect or offensive because they appear to have no legitimate vocation, place of residence, responsibilities, or financial concerns. Nevertheless, the Tewas generally treat visitors with patience and courtesy. Most recognize that many Anglos genuinely admire and respect Tewa culture, and they are proud that people travel from all over the country to see Tewa performances.

In order to establish acceptable behavior for interacting with tourists, the Tewas needed to define the role of tourist in their own terms, finding a place for these outsiders within their system of classification. Primarily through performance and humor, the Tewas have indeed placed tourists within their ordered world. They also have developed a clear concept of what is proper and what is improper behavior for visitors.

Tewa Perceptions of Tourists

During the 1920s, the Fred Harvey Indian Detours regularly brought tourists under the gaze of Tewa people, who looked upon the outsiders with curiosity and amusement. One retired tour guide remembered the Tewas as the most gracious, polite, and hospitable of all the Pueblo groups, but even so, she occasionally saw Tewa women giggle about the tourists' clothing or behavior.

Ever since the days of the detours, Tewa Indians have been categorizing Anglo visitors and comically imitating them. In the middle of a ritual performance, Tewa men may appear in the plaza dressed outlandishly as tourists. During a 1974 San Ildefonso dance, for example, a man walked into the plaza wearing a wig, a pink pillbox hat, high heels, a dress, and a mink coat. This gawky figure aroused hearty laughter, especially when "she" fussed over two baby dolls strapped in cradleboards, mimicking the patronizing airs of some tourists. By exaggerating what seems strange or funny about tourists, the Tewas bring them symbolically into their world.

Tewas think that tourists from "back East" are the most ignorant about New Mexico Indians. One Nambe man said, with a twinkle in his eye, that "back East" was anywhere east of the Pecos River. He added that most Easterners believe that all Indians ride horses, wear buckskins, hunt buffalo, and otherwise fit the Hollywood image of the Plains Indian warrior. It seems to many Tewa Indians that eastern tourists prefer the Comanche and buffalo dances because in them the Tewas match the Plains Indian image by wearing feathered war bonnets, buckskins, or buffalo headdresses.

Another group of tourists identified by the Tewas is that from Texas. Tewas stereotype most Texans as loud, pushy, and rich. In 1968, during a matachines dance at Santa Clara, four men wearing cowboy hats, western shirts, jeans, and boots rushed boisterously into the dance plaza, acting as if they were drunk. Members of the audience referred to them as "tejanos" (personal communication, Luther Lyon). During the 1960s and 1970s, the Tewas occasionally impersonated another group, the "hippies." Long-haired and sandal-shod, hippies stood out from other tourists. Occasionally, they startled the Tewas by jumping up to join in a dance. Like all tourists, the hippies asked many questions about Indian culture, but they seemed endlessly curious about peyote and other hallucinogenic plants, wrongly assuming that all Indians use them regularly.

The ski enthusiast, the ecology buff, and a growing list of other types of tourists have become objects of Tewa burlesque. The Tewas continually create new characters, parodying them more often during the winter and spring ritual performances than during the summer tourist season, perhaps because they do not want to insult large groups of visitors. Tourist impersonations are inside jokes.

The Tewa view of Anglo visitors is also revealed in their arts and crafts. In the

1960s, Anna Maria Vigil, an artist from Tesuque, began making humorous clay figures of Anglo tourists (fig. 28). The female figurines are heavily made up, with bright red lips, cheeks, and fingernails. Black lines up the backs of their legs depict stocking seams. They wear cloth skirts and lacy petticoats and carry leather purses. Their most dramatic feature is an exaggeratedly high, prominent bosom. The male tourist figurines have beards, eye glasses, and hats. Both males and females stand ready to snap a picture with their small wooden cameras.

Some tourist behaviors annoy the Tewas more than others. Because they generally consider direct personal questions to be rude, even during conversations among themselves, it is easy to see why Tewas often complain about tourists' inquisitiveness. They say that tourists' questions, many of which seem irrelevant or too personal, are especially troublesome during a village ritual event when they tend to disrupt the Tewas' concentration on the ritual. Some fear that if they are seen talking to tourists during a ritual, others will think that they are giving away esoteric information. One Tewa woman said, "If they would just listen and watch instead of ask questions, they would begin to understand."

To cope with the inquisitive tourists, many Tewa Indians have developed techniques for distancing themselves politely. Response to a question may be very short or "I don't know," after which the Tewa may turn away from the visitor. Eye contact is usually avoided throughout the interchange, and if questioning persists, some Tewas will simply refuse to acknowledge the tourist's presence.

Another common complaint arises from the tourist's desire to take photographs. Some Tewa Indians resent being photographed because it violates their sense of privacy, and some object that the visitor will reproduce the picture for commercial gain. Because they believe that taking photographs is a special privilege, not a right, the Tewas sell photo permits during certain village rituals. A permit gives the visitor freedom to photograph the performance group, but permission to take other shots around the village must be sought from the individual subject or property owner.

Occasionally, visitors give offense by refusing an invitation to feast in the home of a Tewa family. Usually, only a few tourists can be invited to eat during any one ritual performance, but the Tewas serve as many guests as possible. As soon as one group of relatives, friends, or visitors leaves the table, it is cleared and set for the next hungry group. The feasting is a time for Tewa women to show off their cooking skills and hospitality—and also a time for testing visitors. Will they eat Indian food? Can they swallow hot chile stew? Are the men "macho" enough to eat hot chile without perspiration or tears? Refusing to eat is a great insult, but enthusiastic consumption of spicy hot stew and freshly baked bread symbolizes friendship. The Tewas are proud of their foods and their tradition of sharing with outsiders.

Figure 28. Two clay figurines by Anna Maria Vigil, photographed in a museum display, reveal a Tewa artist's perception of Anglo tourists. (Courtesy Girard Foundation collection in the Museum of International Folk Art, a unit of the Museum of New Mexico; photo by Deborah Flynn.)

Some Tewas smile at the Anglo's propensity to overuse polite words and phrases, such as "please" and "thank you." They also feel that Anglo tourists introduce themselves too quickly. The Tewas generally give people time to feel at ease before identifying them, whereas most tourists become uncomfortable if everyone is not introduced immediately. Furthermore, the Tewas perceive most Anglos as impatient. Before a ritual performance begins, tourists ask repeatedly, "When is the dance going to start?" And then, "Are they going to do this same dance all day, or will there be something else happening?"

Anglo behavior toward dogs also strikes many Tewas as odd. Most Tewa village dogs are kept outdoors as scavengers, and it is quite acceptable to kick a dog out of the way during a village ritual. When an outsider picks up and fondles a village dog, the behavior seems bizarre, if not disgusting.

If tourists sometimes behave strangely, by Tewa standards, they are also recognized as economically important: they are the primary consumers of Indian arts and crafts. Many Tewa families depend on tourist dollars for at least part of their livelihood. In the mid-1970s, leaders of the American Indian Movement (AIM) urged all Native Americans to boycott the tourist industry on the grounds that it exploited Indians. The Tewas did not subscribe to this idea, and in the June 13, 1975, edition of the Santa Fe *New Mexican,* Governor Lucario Padilla of Santa Clara responded:

> The position of the Santa Clara Pueblo…is that we cannot and will not condone the attitude the American Indian Movement has taken regarding tourism.… We realize the tremendous impact of the tourist trade upon the economy of the people within our pueblo, therefore, we cannot possibly bar the door without serious repercussions on the ability of our pueblo to earn a living. But, we must reiterate that anyone entering our pueblo as visitors must be aware of the responsibilities that accompany their roles as guests and act accordingly.

In spite of occasional frustrations over tourist behavior, some Tewa families develop solid and lifelong friendships with visitors who repeatedly return to New Mexico. For the Tewa family who befriends them, the term used for these returning visitors changes from *tourist* to *white* or *Anglo friend.* Sometimes they become confidants because they are safe outsiders and not members of the Tewa community. They may hear confidential stories not shared with Tewa neighbors or relatives, perhaps complaints about family members. Unfortunately, this role has led some Anglos to characterize the Tewa people as gossipers. It has also resulted in cases of inappropriate Anglo involvement in Tewa family affairs.

Usually, Tewa Indians will forgive outsiders for social blunders because they understand the limitations of cross-cultural communication. They see even their

Anglo friends as not entirely able to comprehend their ways. At most, the Tewas hope to communicate that they are a proud and strong cultural group with traditions that set them apart from Anglos, Hispanics, and other Native Americans.

Tourist Perceptions of Tewas

Anglos often develop an over-romantic attitude toward Tewas and other Pueblo Indians. Many assume that all Pueblo Indians are supreme natural artists, mystics, and ecologists. Some Anglos also see Indians as victims of an oppressive nation and feel guilty about past and present government policies toward Native Americans. Perhaps because of this romanticism and guilt, Anglos may place Pueblo Indians on a cultural pedestal. But Tewas and other Indian people, of course, are not perfect and should not be expected to live up to the images and ideals of Anglos.

The Fred Harvey Company developed the image of the Pueblo Indian as artist as part of its Southwest promotion (see Frost 1980). The concept was further perpetuated by a group of Anglo artists and intellectuals who came to the Southwest during the 1920s and 1930s. The romance of the natural environment and the Hispanic and Pueblo villages so attracted some that they established permanent residence in the area. Erna Fergusson (1936:377–78), an author and contemporary of this artistic group, described the extent of its identification with the Indians:

> Witter Bynner bought and wore and hung on his friends a famous collection of Indian jewelry. Alice Corbin introduced the velvet Navaho blouse …even blankets were the approved costume. Everybody had a pet pueblo, a pet Indian, a pet craft….Jane Henderson made a record by living at Santa Clara all winter and learning a whole repertoire of Indian songs. Mary Austin discovered and ordered her life to the beat of the Amerindian rhythm. Carlos Vierra and Jesse Nusbaum designed the state museum along lines of the pueblo missions.… It was obligatory to go to every pueblo dance. Failure to appear on a sunny roof on every saint's day marked one as soulless and without taste.

The artists admired the Indians as outstanding "natural" artists. The painter John Sloan and the writer Oliver La Farge wrote, "The Indian is a born artist; possessing a capacity for discipline and careful work, and a fine sense of line and rhythm, which seems to be inherent in the Mongoloid peoples" (Sloan and La Farge n.d.:5). Artist Marsden Hartley wrote, "I want merely, then, esthetic recognition in full of the contribution of the redman as artist, as one of the finest artists of time; the poetic redman ceremonialist, celebrant of the universe as he sees it, and master among masters of the art of symbolic gesture" (Hartley 1920:14). These attitudes encouraged the stereotype of the Pueblo Indians as artists, idealized for their crafts, painting, music, and dance. While the image of the Pueblo Indian as artist began more than sixty years ago, several scholars believe that it continues to flourish (see Frost 1980; Ortiz 1979b:282). The generalization that all Tewas and other Pueblo Indians are innately artistic falsely suggests that a Tewa Indian lacking these attributes somehow does not measure up. It also incorrectly assumes that if their talents are innate, they need not work at their art.

The elaborate ritual life of Pueblo Indians may lead visitors to assume that all members of the community are natural religious mystics. Tewas have a very rich spiritual life, but religious commitment varies and some individuals are minimally involved in the spiritual dimension of the community.

Indian as environmentalist is another stereotype held by some visitors, an idea that probably developed because the Indians do understand the interdependence of ecosystems and many of their rituals do honor nature. But Tewas also participate in a modem technological world. They depend on gasoline and electricity like any other consumers, thus contributing their share to contemporary ecological problems.

Idealizing the Indian cannot reverse past mistakes. Romanticism does not lead to understanding but encourages unrealistic expectations and stereotyping. Open-mindedness without preconceptions will gain the visitor a more accurate glimpse into Tewa culture.

Hosts and Guests

The Tewa Indians, having dealt with tourists for years, are often more patient with visitors than the visitors are with one another. There is a tendency for tourists to look at one another with scorn. Few of them like to admit that they are tourists or that they are not "in the know," but, not understanding the rules of Pueblo society, they do sometimes make social errors and sometimes look foolish. Many tourists hope to get "backstage" for a privileged look at what others seldom get to see. For a few, the honor of sharing a meal at a Tewa home satisfies this desire. But some tourists, to the annoyance of their hosts and the embarrassment of other visitors, wander about the village peering into the windows of private homes or trying to gain entrance to the kivas. Tourists have even been known to wander out into the corn fields and help themselves to fresh produce.

Common sense is not always enough to guide people in cross-cultural interactions. That which the guest regards as polite behavior may be considered rude by the host. Visitors to Tewa villages can avoid the most common misunderstandings by observing the following suggestions:

Avoid asking Indians to discuss religious or personal matters.

Watch the ritual dances quietly from the edge of the plaza.

Do not sit in chairs that you yourself have not brought, and do not stand in front of people who are seated.

Observe the rules for photography, sound recording, sketching, and note taking. If no signs are posted, ask a villager.

Do not climb on or enter the kivas.

Remember that Tewa ritual performances are religious occasions; dress conservatively.

If invited to a meal in a Tewa home, do not insult the host by refusing.

Visitors at Tewa village ritual performances should be wary of the ritual clowns. Because they deal with outsiders through humor, making people look foolish is part of their job. A visitor who is approached by a clown with his playful antics should simply try to be a good sport.

The visitor who comes to the village with an open mind will understand more about the Tewas than will the person who comes looking for a stereotyped image. A tourist who relaxes and quietly observes the ritual activities is more likely to appreciate the unique beauty of the movement, songs, and colorful costumes in what can be an extraordinarily moving experience.

CHAPTER FIVE
KEEPING THE RITUALS ALIVE

Village ritual performance is perhaps the single most important expression of Tewa cultural continuity. While their material culture and economic activities have become increasingly "Americanized," the Tewas' commitment to traditional village performances has remained unshaken by years of involvement in theatrical shows for tourists. Even Pojoaque and Nambe, the villages that have suffered the greatest cultural disruption, are reviving some of their ritual performances with the help of Tewa elders from neighboring pueblos. Such conviction surprises many outsiders. Why are the Tewas so dedicated to their ritual calendar of village performances? How have they kept their village rituals vital in the face of pressures to conform to the larger Hispanic and Anglo societies? Moreover, how do they perceive the differences between theatrical and ritual performance? And what is the future of Tewa performance?

The Tewas' commitment to their religious rituals became most violently apparent in the Pueblo Revolt of 1680, for which Spanish interference in village rituals was among the primary causes. The Spaniards had punished the Tewas for participating in native rituals, raiding their kivas and destroying their ritual objects. They forced the Indians to attend mass and work for the missionaries. During the revolt, the Pueblo Indians killed twenty-one out of thirty-three Spanish missionaries and successfully, if temporarily, drove the Spaniards from the area. After the reconquest, missionaries were never again so intolerant of the native ritual performances.

A more recent example dates to the 1920s, when John Collier took his delegations of Tewa and other Pueblo Indians to lobby in Washington, D.C. Among their primary concerns were several circulars sent by Charles H. Burke, commissioner of Indian affairs, to all superintendents of Indian reservations throughout the United States, suggesting that most forms of Indian ritual dance be discouraged or banned. Although his recommendations never became government policy, Burke caused a great furor among the Pueblo Indians. Some encouraged their Anglo friends to write letters and articles in defense of the Indian's right to dance. One of the most insightful of these appeared in *The New Republic,* in which Elizabeth Sergeant (1923:357) wrote:

> The reason why certain powers, deeply influential in Indian life, are out to "get" Indian dances is not that they are harmful, but that so long as they continue, the Indian cannot be transformed into a white man…with the dances, will die Indian costume and handicraft and decorative symbolism, Indian rhythm and music and song, Indian worship and communal consciousness. Then will every Indian surely prefer the Y.M.C.A. to the kiva, the cornet to the tombe, and the movies to the Deer Dance.

Opposition to Indian dance is no longer a political issue, yet these earlier conflicts taught the Tewas not to take for granted the right to perform their ritual dances. They learned that commitment to their village ritual performances is simultaneously a commitment to religious freedom. The ritual performance as a whole, with its multitude of related meanings and messages, is the most potent symbol or public expression of the people's refusal to become anything other than Tewa. Other aspects of their lives have changed and will continue to do so, but so long as the people hold their village performances, they remain Tewa and are not swept into the mainstream of contemporary American life. Simply put, the Tewas are committed to their village performances because they are committed to the survival of their culture and society.

Over the years of contact with successive waves of non-Pueblo peoples, the Tewa Indians have developed innovative yet conservative techniques for keeping their ritual performance cycle intact. In the early years of coexistence with the Spaniards, the Tewas and other Pueblo Indians practiced what some anthropologists call "compartmentalization" (Spicer 1954:665–670; Dozier 1961:94). By adopting but deliberately practicing separately (that is, keeping in separate "compartments") certain aspects of Spanish culture, the Pueblos managed to keep the borrowed traits as additions to, rather than replacements for, their native customs. An example is the separate practice of Catholic and kiva rituals. With the relaxation of Spanish policies, the Tewas began more freely to combine, recombine, and juxtapose the foreign with the native. Yet, they continued to practice a cognitive form of compartmentalization by remaining aware of the origins of most borrowed elements. They are masters at discriminately selecting foreign objects and practices and interlacing them with existing Tewa traditions, all the while maintaining a clear distinction between what came from "us" and what came from "them." The ability to selectively integrate aspects of other cultures into their own has served the Tewas well in creating their own ceremonials by combining Anglo theatrical practices with Tewa notions of ritual performance.

The results of this selective interlacing of cultural features can also be seen in many village performances. The Comanche dance, for example, compares with other Tewa dances in having a formation of two long parallel lines. The women wear typical Tewa costumes, carry ears of corn and sprigs of evergreens, and contain their movements in Tewa style. The music resembles that of the Tewa buffalo dance, and the whole performance is a gesture of thanksgiving, a celebration of life, and a prayer for community health and prosperity. At the same time, the male dancers and singers wear costumes knowingly adopted from the Plains Indians. Some of the song texts include Comanche words. Since the Comanche dance is frequently performed at patron saint's day celebrations, a Catholic element also appears; at least some of the performance is done before a statue of the village's patron saint. The people remain well aware of the Tewa, Comanche, and Spanish Catholic sources of the dance's symbols.

A Catholic mass at a Tewa village church may show the interlacing of a few Tewa elements into a "foreign" event. The altar is often decorated with traditional Tewa rain or cloud symbols. The chalice may be made of pottery painted with Tewa designs, and some of the priest's robes may be embroidered with native symbols. During the 1970s, the priest at San Juan began saying parts of the mass in Tewa and printing Tewa translations of prayers for the congregation. During a patron saint's day celebration or on Christmas Eve, Tewa dancers sometimes perform in the village church.

The conscious borrowing and combining of foreign practices and symbols most easily occurs when a group has a strong sense of its own culture, and cultural self-consciousness is only intensified by contact with foreigners. Perhaps because the Tewas have for so long dealt with so many outsiders who do things differently and hold different values, they have been challenged and forced to sharpen their definition of themselves and their world. Interaction with tourists can especially stimulate cultural self-consciousness because the tourist's inquisitiveness demands that the host group examine and be able to articulate its beliefs and practices. Much of what was taken for granted must be systematically rationalized. Even the brief explanations prepared for theatrical performances outside the villages force the Tewas to think about and explain some of the meanings behind their traditions and beliefs.

A traditional principle of secrecy is another Tewa device for keeping the village performances vital and meaningful. The Tewas believe that there is power in the esoteric and that sacred information which becomes public may lose its power. Members of the village religious societies never discuss their activities with nonmembers, and in some cases, if a nonmember villager inadvertently witnesses a society's private rituals, he or she will be obliged to join the group. Thus, the esoteric knowledge stays within the religious society and retains its power. Tewa youths occasionally complain that their elders are unwilling to tell them about religious practices and beliefs. This intergenerational secrecy stems from the idea that young people must demonstrate maturity and responsibility before learning about such matters.

Because the Tewas already valued secrecy, they found it a ready tool to use against outsiders. While the Catholic priests said mass, the Tewas secretly kept their native religion alive. Later, anthropologists who came to study that religion met with frustration upon finding the Tewas extremely close-mouthed. Tourists also face silence when they question Tewas about private religious matters.

Peer pressure helps sustain the secrecy principle. Tewas sometimes gossip about people who talk too much with outsiders about religious matters. Gossip also keeps Tewas from behaving disrespectfully during village rituals. For example, people will talk about someone who is obviously intoxicated during a village performance, and the clowns may publicly ridicule the individual.

The selective interlacing of native and foreign traits reflects the Tewas' innovations in making room for new patterns and symbols, while secrecy and social control represent the conservative side of Tewa response to culture contact. The combination of these mechanisms enables the Tewas to keep their village rituals vital.

At first glance, one might assume that the Tewas' participation in theatrical productions is a sign that they are abandoning their religious foundations and becoming a more secular society. Quite the opposite is true. When Tewas compare theatrical shows with village rituals, they often insist that both kinds of performances contain the same fundamental meanings. Performing in a theatrical event can promote growth, fertility, rainfall, and life and can bring blessing to the people and the village, if only the Tewas dance and sing "from the heart." So long as the performers are sincerely committed to the gestures and words of the songs, the meanings remain intact. As one Tewa man expressed it, "You've still got to dance with your whole heart because the songs and dance still are sacred and bring beauty, no matter if you dance here or out there."

The Tewas do not segregate that which a Western thinker might consider to be sacred from that which would be considered secular. They have long celebrated both in ritual performance, juxtaposing the solemn and the humorous, the serious and the absurd, the mystical and the mundane, the ancient and the contemporary. For them, there is no contradiction in adapting segments of their ritual dances for secular, commercial theatrical events.

From the Tewa perspective, the theatrical differs from the ritual not in meaning but in form. Theatrical productions are kept separate in space and time: they are not held in the sacred village plazas and kivas, and they are not part of the native ritual calendar. Their form is distinct in that only segments of songs and dances are performed and the audience is primarily non-Tewa. These changes in form not only are necessary adjustments made for theatrical productions but also stand as markers that commercial tourist shows are different from village ritual events, despite their shared higher-order meanings. The separateness of the theatrical performances, both cognitively and in practice, prevents them from influencing or altering the ritual performances.

In short, the Tewa Pueblo Indians can take part in theatrical productions without destroying their ancient ritual cycle because they maintain a strong commitment to their rituals as indicators of cultural survival; because they respond to other cultures creatively, selectively, and conservatively; and because they perceive the two types of performances as differing in form but not in meaning. The Tewa Indians are neither great resistors of change nor victims of secularization. Rather, they respond to contact situations with their own form of creative ingenuity.

During the first quarter of the twentieth century, Anglo writers predicted that it was only a matter of time before the Pueblo Indians' elaborate ritual performances would cease to exist. Some cited Nambe and Pojoaque, whose performance cycles had virtually died out, as examples of what was bound to happen to other villages. These dire predictions proved wrong. The other Tewa villages have a vigorous ritual performance system in the 1980s, and even Nambe and Pojoaque have shown dramatic signs of recovery during the past twenty years. I would predict that because village ritual performances are such central and important symbols of Tewa culture, they will thrive rather than diminish as the world around the Tewas continues to change. The future of Southwestern theatrical productions is less clear, but at least two trends will probably continue: the rise of semiprofessional dance troupes and a movement toward greater Indian control of theatrical shows.

As commercial productions became common in the Southwest, Tewa participants began forming semiprofessional dance troupes, the leadership of which generally fell on the oldest male, who took the role of singer and drummer while the younger members danced. Today, about eight Tewa dance troupes perform regularly for theatrical productions, their membership changing from time to time. Some groups consist of children, others of adults; a few travel considerable distances to perform outside the Southwest. The most widely traveled Tewa troupe in recent years is a group of teenagers who call themselves the San Juan Indian Youth Dancers. Beginning as an Alateen organization, part of a national program designed to help children of alcoholics cope with their social, emotional, and substance abuse problems, the group decided in 1975 to form a dance troupe and perform at schools, hospitals, and centers for recovering alcoholics. They have also presented segments of Tewa dances and songs at ceremonials, arts and crafts fairs, and festivals as far away as Toronto, Mexico City, and Washington, D.C. Their performing not only promotes cultural pride and helps ensure the preservation of Tewa dance but also helps prevent substance abuse among the members. The San Juan Indian Youth Dancers are successfully using tradition to cope with a contemporary social problem.

Semiprofessional dance troupes will probably increase among the Tewas, primarily because many people enjoy performing and traveling and welcome the opportunity to earn extra money. Although members of these groups complain that some people resent the attention they receive from outsiders, they also describe Southwestern theatrical productions as exciting events where they enjoy socializing with other Indians. I believe, however, that these groups are unlikely to be composed of full-time professional entertainers because there are no models for such a role in traditional Tewa culture and there are a limited number of events for them to participate in.

As ceremonials wane and arts and crafts fairs wax profitable, we can see a corresponding movement away from Anglo-inspired events to those conceived, organized, and run by Tewas themselves. If Tewa-organized ceremonials were a first step toward the creation of tourist events more acceptable to the Tewas, arts and crafts fairs such as the ENIPC Artist and Craftsman Show are another step in that direction. The future of Southwestern theatrical productions involving Tewa performance is increasingly in the hands of the Tewas themselves as they exercise greater control over what tourists may see of their performance traditions.

Though Tewa-organized theatrical productions may flourish, village rituals will remain the more important kind of performance. Through them, the Tewa people can fully express their perceptions of the world and its beauty, humor, and vitality. The gentle, subtle movements, elaborate costumes, and strong voices singing poetically create a magical experience dedicated to the search for and renewal of life.

> Our ancestors used to tell us.... Go there to the dance and ask the gods there to give good life—regain your life and make your life a longer life.... You go there like to go to church.... To ask the spirits to give us better life—a longer life—regain life.

Figure 29. Untitled © *1966 by Santiago Romero (Mateo Romero's father), watercolor on board, 24 x 30.*

Figure 30. Four Worlds, Four Tides © *2000 by Mateo Romero, mixed media, 48 x 72.*

The More Predictable Dates
for Tewa Village Ritual Performances

Exact dates can be given only for those village ritual performances associated with the Catholic calendar. Other performance dates vary from year to year. Visitors can sometimes find out the less predictable performance dates by telephoning the office of the governor of each pueblo.

January 6	Performances at some Tewa villages
January 23	Buffalo and Comanche dances at San Ildefonso for patron saint's day
Easter Sunday	Performances at some Tewa villages
June 13	Performances at some Tewa villages
June 24	Buffalo dance and Comanche or green corn dance at San Juan for patron saint's day
August 12	Blue corn, harvest, and other dances at Santa Clara for patron saint's day
October 4	Yellow corn or elk dance at Nambe for patron saint's day
November 12	Comanche or deer dance at Tesuque for patron saint's day
December 12	Performances at Pojoaque for patron saint's day
December 24	Matachines dance at San Juan
December 25	Performances at some Tewa villages
December 26	Turtle dance at San Juan

A Guide to Identifying Tewa Dances

The following descriptions should help visitors recognize and identify some of the more common Tewa dances. I mention here only the most distinctive features of each dance because I have already described the general kinds of choreography, costumes, and music that all the dances share.

Tewa dances popularly known by the same English names are sometimes performed very differently from one village to another. What the San Juan Tewas call the yellow corn dance may not resemble the Nambe yellow corn dance. To describe every dance in all its variations would be difficult and confusing, so I have chosen instead to describe each dance as I saw it performed at one particular village or theatrical production between 1973 and 1981. Each of the following descriptions applies to the village noted in parentheses after the name of the dance. Where variations are known for other villages, I mention them very briefly.

BASKET DANCE (San Juan). Symbolizing fertility, crops, and the female, the basket dance has two parts: a slow, standing dance and a faster section in which the line of women kneels and scrapes notched sticks over baskets while the line of men faces them and ântegeh in place. The performers sing as they dance, with no drum accompaniment or separate male chorus. Men's costumes include a headdress of yucca stalks and three upright feathers (see figs. 6 and 26). Each woman carries a basket in her left hand, wears a heavy woven manta, or shawl, over her black manta-dress, and has her hair parted so that half is gathered and tied at each side of her head.

Santa Clara also performs a version of the basket dance, but the men wear squash-blossom headdresses rather than headdresses of yucca stalks.

BLUE CORN DANCE (Santa Clara). This agricultural dance is performed by the winter moiety for Santa Clara's patron saint's day celebration every August 12. Its basic choreographic formation is two parallel lines of alternating male and female dancers, who are accompanied by a drummer and a chorus of male singers. The women wear elaborately carved tablita headdresses, often painted in bright colors; white manta-dresses with a white blouse underneath; and brightly colored, lace-edged shawls. The men wear squash-blossom headdresses, white shirts, and white crocheted leggings with their kilts. This dance was introduced to the Santa Clara Tewas by a Hopi-Tewa, and it resembles the Hopi butterfly dance.

BOW DANCE (Tesuque). To express a hunting and game animal theme, male dancers wear large, white, animal-hide capes over their right shoulders and carry bows in their left hands. They form a single line and simply ântegeh in place, occasionally pivoting to change facing direction. The dancers sing as they dance, repeatedly moving the bow from a horizontal to a nearly vertical position and from hip to shoulder level. Sometimes this dance is called the *bow and arrow dance,* although arrows are not carried.

A small group of San Ildefonso women sometimes performs the bow dance, one of the few instances in which women's voices can be heard, since there are no male singers to overpower them.

BUFFALO DANCE (San Ildefonso). There are many versions of Tewa buffalo dances; Kurath and Garcia (1970:199) identified five types based on the number of buffalo and other game animals represented. At San Ildefonso, the buffalo dance, also called the *game animal* dance, begins with a dawn ceremony and features two buffalo, a game mother, two antelope, and dozens of deer. As many as forty additional side dancers, equal numbers of men and women, appear in some years, with the male-side dancers wearing one-horned headdresses.

Each animal represented has a particular movement style and choreographic pattern. The antelope dart about with small running steps; the deer walk with deeply bent knees, leaning on two sticks held as forelegs (see figs. 15 and 33); and the movements of the buffalo and game mother include slow meandering walks and quick steps in place with frequent pivots. The San Ildefonso game mother traditionally wears a red floral-patterned shawl with long fringe over her black manta-dress. The antelope and deer wear antler headdresses, and the buffalo, bison headdresses (see fig. 25). All the performers wear black face paint. Several drummers and a chorus of male singers accompany the dancers.

Because bison are associated with hunting and with the snow needed for spring moisture, buffalo dances are traditionally held in winter, though segments may often be seen during summer theatrical productions. San Ildefonso regularly holds its buffalo dance on January 23 in honor of the village's patron saint. Santa Clara, San Juan, and Nambe frequently present other versions of the buffalo dance.

BULL DANCE (Santa Clara). The program for the 1973 Puye Cliffs ceremonial described the bull dance as "the Pueblo's [sic] tribute to the bull for providing them with food and other basic materials." Its primary choreographic formation is a single line of alternating male and female dancers. The men, who wear small horns and layers of evergreen branches on their heads, each carry a three-foot staff topped with evergreens and feathers. During one section of the dance, they lean on their staffs as they ântegeh in place. The women are dressed in white manta-dresses, with lace-trimmed shawls pinned over their right shoulders. The group is accompanied by one or more drummers and a chorus of male singers.

BUTTERFLY DANCE (San Juan). The butterfly dance connotes spring, fertility, war and peace, and the female. At San Juan, the dance begins with a *wasa,* or weaving section, in which small groups of dancers standing shoulder-to-shoulder travel with short diagonal steps to one side and then to the other, facing forward all the while. Because some groups begin by traveling to the right and others to the left, they create an illusion of weaving from side to side as they slowly progress sideways and forward. The wasa is followed by a series of male and female partner performances. The partners move backwards and away from each other with small jumps, then pivot around to travel backwards but towards each other.

The woman butterfly dancer wears a white manta-dress and two rows of feathers that stand out from her back, from the shoulders to below the waist, representing butterfly wings (see fig. 27). Her partner wears an otter fur bib over his white shirt, a kilt, crocheted leggings, a rain sash, and a headband with three large feathers attached. He carries a tomahawk in his right hand and swings it as he dances.

Santa Clara Tewas also perform the butterfly dance, but rather than begin with the wasa, they start with a counterclockwise circle dance. Nambe Tewas perform a version of this dance, but they refer to it as the *spring dance.*

CLOUD DANCE (San Juan). Also called the *three times* or the *corn maiden dance,* the cloud dance is usually held in late winter or early spring—before spring planting—because of its association with agriculture, weather control, and fertility. At San Juan, the dance begins with a wasa section, as described for the butterfly dance. This is followed by a series of single-line performances in which the male dancers sing as they dance and one man beats the drum. With each appearance of the male dancers, two different women perform. They wear elaborate headdresses made of twelve eagle feathers arranged in a fan on top of the head. The women carry an ear of corn in each hand and wear black manta-dresses with a white blouse underneath, along with brightly colored, lace-trimmed shawls (see fig. 18). The men dance shirtless but cover their chests, backs, arms, and lower legs with black body paint. White paint is applied to their waists, hands, and upper legs.

San Ildefonso also performs a version of the cloud dance.

COMANCHE DANCE (San Ildefonso). Every Tewa village has a version of the Comanche dance in its repertoire. One Tewa consultant told me that the songs contain some words believed to be of Comanche origin and that the dance is reminiscent of a time when some Comanche warriors were "sent home crying" after a battle with the Tewa Indians. The San Ildefonso Tewas present the Comanche dance along with a buffalo dance on their patron saint's day, January 23.

Male Comanche dancers concoct gaudy costumes that might include feathered war bonnets, fringed buckskin pants, breechcloths, beaded leather vests, feathered bustles, a variety of kilts, bone breast plates, and elaborate body-and-face paint (see figs. 9, 13, and 22). Each man carries a banner in his left hand and a rattle in his right. The women wear black manta-dresses or colorful cotton dresses with lace-trimmed shawls. They also wear headbands with three large feathers attached at either side and hold three feathers in each hand. The dancers file into the plaza in two lines, in which men and women alternate. To the accompaniment of several male drummers and singers, the women step lightly in place with slight pivots from side to side as the men repeatedly cross in front of them with larger, more exaggerated movements.

CORN GRINDING DANCE (Santa Clara). The corn grinding dance may challenge some visitors' definition of dance because it simply features several girls grinding corn as a group of men sings. The girls, usually between eight and fourteen years old, kneel and rock forward and back as they use traditional stone grinding tools. Each wears a feather in her hair, a manta-dress or print dress, and a bright, solid-color, lace-trimmed shawl.

CORN MAIDEN DANCE. See CLOUD DANCE.

DEER DANCE (San Juan). At some Tewa villages, deer dancers are included in the buffalo or game animal dance. The San Juan deer dance, however, features a long line of young male deer dancers without buffalo. It is a winter dance associated with hunting success and masculinity. The dancers wear kilts, white crocheted leggings, white shirts, and headdresses of deer antlers and yucca stalks. The performance begins with an evening prelude dance, followed the next morning by a dawn ceremony in which the deer enter the village from the east. Throughout the performance, the dancers are accompanied by a drummer and a chorus of male singers. Tesuque and Santa Clara Tewas also present versions of this dance.

DOG DANCE (San Juan). Some Tewas claim that this dance honors the dog as a helpful companion to man. Others say that it symbolizes the role of the Tewa male as warrior and family protector. The men wear black pants, black shirts, and headdresses consisting of a single row of feathers running from the top of the head down the back to below the waist. The women wear black manta-dresses, white blouses, and lace-trimmed shawls over their shoulders. Each male dancer has one end of a cord or long woven sash attached to his belt; a female dancer holds the other end. Throughout the dance, the men lead and the women follow, holding the cord loosely. A small group of male singers and one or more drummers accompany the dancers.

The Nambe Tewas have a version of this dance in their repertoire, but for reasons unknown to me, they call it the *snake dance*.

EAGLE DANCE (Santa Clara). Tewas associate the eagle with rain, thunder, lightning, and curative powers, honoring the bird in this dance. The dancers, all men, each wear a white cap with a beak, a row of eagle feathers down each arm, and a row across the back. The choreography includes many deep knee bends, or squats, and frequent pivots executed with the arms held out to suggest a bird repeatedly soaring and landing. The dancers are accompanied by a drummer and male singers.

The villages of San lldefonso, San Juan, Nambe, and Tesuque also have young men who perform versions of the eagle dance.

ELK DANCE (Nambe). The only Tewa village where the elk dance is currently performed is Nambe, which holds the dance on October 4 every seventh year. The elk dance is a men's dance associated with hunting success and an abundance of game. The dancers are accompanied by a chorus of male singers and one or more drummers. Each dancer wears a white shirt, a kilt, white crocheted leggings, and an antler headdress. The basic formation is two parallel lines, but there is a special choreographic feature in which the dancers exit into the kiva. They all run counterclockwise around the top of the circular kiva, and after each circle, one "animal" descends into the kiva. If there are twenty-five dancers, the last to descend has to circle twenty-five times.

HARVEST DANCE (San lldefonso). The San lldefonso harvest dance is usually held in early September because it is an agricultural dance offering thanks for the summer's bounty. It is performed by both men and women to the accompaniment of a drummer and male chorus. The women wear black manta-dresses, red woven sashes, and turquoise-blue tablita headdresses. They carry evergreens in each hand, and most perform barefooted. The men wear kilts, shell bandoleers, rain sashes, and moccasins. They cover their chests, backs, and lower legs with black paint and their waists and hands with white paint.

There are two basic sections to the choreography. First, a man carrying a large, feather-topped, woven banner leads the two lines of dancers counterclockwise around the entire dance area (see fig. 7). Then, the two lines face each other and the dancers perform numerous changes of formation, always returning to their original places in the lines. After several hours of dancing, the participants form a tight circle near the kiva while other villagers toss food to them in appreciation for the performance and for the harvest.

The summer moiety at Santa Clara performs its harvest dance on August 12. San Juan Tewas sometimes present a harvest dance in the fall, but the women dancers do not wear tablitas.

HOOP DANCE (San Ildefonso). This showy, crowd-pleasing dance has no direct connection to the traditional Tewa ritual calendar, and its origins have been debated. Some Tewas say that it was invented by a Taos family. The dance is performed by young men who have learned the acrobatics of keeping hoops whirling around their arms and legs as they execute quick footwork over, under, and through additional hoops. The action can be very exciting. Currently, several San Ildefonso boys perform the hoop dance at theatrical productions. They generally wear breechcloths and some type of feathered headdress. Hoop dancers are accompanied by a drum, but no songs.

HOPI CORN DANCE (Santa Clara). Tewa consultants say that this agricultural dance is borrowed from the Hopi Pueblo Indians. As in other Tewa corn dances, fertility and the female are central themes. The Hopi corn dance, however, can be distinguished by its costumes. The women wear tablitas, black manta-dresses, and lace-trimmed shawls, as they do in many other dances, but they also wear black headbands with black fringe that covers their eyes. The men's costumes are also unusual: they include a black shirt with many colored ribbons at the shoulders and a red scarf tied at the side of the head. Accompaniment is provided by a drummer and several male singers. San Ildefonso also performs a version of the Hopi corn dance.

MATACHINES DANCE (San Juan). This dance, performed in San Juan each year on December 24 and 25, is believed to be of Spanish and Christian origins, taught to the Indians by the early Franciscan missionaries. Its movements and accompaniment are not typical of Tewa dance and music. The dancers execute skips, hops, swing kicks, and polka steps in many intricate choreographic patterns while visiting Hispanic musicians play tunes traceable to sixteenth-century Europe on the violin and guitar.

The matachines dancers include men who wear black pants and vests trimmed in beadwork, beaded moccasins, scarves over their mouths, and black fringe over their eyes. On their heads they wear miters from which long colorful streamers flow down their backs (see fig. 21). One young girl, called Malinche, dressed in a white sweater over a white or solid-color dress, dances among the matachines or with the male soloist, called Monanca. He is distinguished from the matachines by his conical crown topped with a small crucifix. A small boy wearing a bull hide and carrying two sticks as forelegs takes the role of *el toro,* the bull. There are also two clowns or *abuelos* ("grandfathers"), who wear masks and carry whips.

San Ildefonso also holds a matachines dance on December 25, similar to the San Juan version. Santa Clara's summer moiety performs its version on the same day. The Santa Clara Malinche wears a tan-colored manta decorated with Tewa symbols, and the accompaniment is provided by drummers and a male chorus. Versions of this dance are performed at other Pueblo and Hispanic villages throughout New Mexico, as well as in some Mexican communities.

NAVAJO DANCE (San Ildefonso). The Navajo dance is a playful burlesque of Navajo behavior as perceived and defined by the Tewas. The dancers wear clothing typical of the Navajos: for the women, velveteen shirts, silver concha belts, and long, gathered skirts; for the men, similar shirts and belts, loose trousers or denim jeans, and Western hats or scarves tied around their heads (see fig. 19). Sometimes Tewa women alone perform the dance, taking both male and female roles. The dancers sing as they dance and are accompanied by a drummer, also clad in Navajo garb. Their movements are typical of other Tewa double-line dances, but sometimes an imitation of a specific Navajo dance is included.

Santa Clara Tewas also perform a Navajo dance in which both men and women take part.

RAIN DANCE (Santa Clara). The rain dance invokes the sun and promotes rain and agricultural success. Usually, it is performed in the spring when the community begins to clear the irrigation ditches. The woman's costume is a white manta-dress, a headdress made of feathers, a flat, curved, wooden disc painted with the colors of the rainbow, and a feather bustle worn at the lower back. Each woman carries a nearly flat basket-plaque edged in orange angora wool. Men are dressed in kilts, white shirts, and white crocheted leggings and carry feather-topped lances or staffs.

After the dancers travel in a circle around the dance area, the men and women stop and face each other to perform, first, a slow section in which the men bend their knees in place as the women repeatedly swing their basket-plaques from side to side in front of their knees. Then follows a faster section in which the men travel towards and away from the women, raising and lowering their lances in a forward motion as they travel. The women remain in place, pivoting from side to side and holding their basket-plaques at eye level.

Kurath and Garcia (1970:26) state that this dance was revived by the Santa

Clara Tewas in 1925. It has also been called the *sun basket dance* or the *sun dance.*

RAINBOW DANCE (Santa Clara). Rainbows are important indicators of rain and agricultural success. In this dance, both men and women carry flat, curved, wooden plaques painted like rainbows, which they move from side to side to create a visual arc. Each dancer wears another rainbow-painted wooden plaque for a headdress. The choreography of this particularly energetic dance includes short, quick, side steps, short leaps from foot to foot, and occasional hops on the same foot. The performers are accompanied by a drummer and male chorus.

SNAKE DANCE. See DOG DANCE.

SPRING DANCE. See BUTTERFLY DANCE.

SPRING SOCIAL DANCE (San Juan). This dance has important associations with fertility and agricultural success. It is typically performed in late winter, in early spring, or on Easter Sunday. In it, a line of men faces a line of women. Each dancer steps sideways, traveling to the head of the line, and then joins the dancer opposite to travel back down between the two lines. Depending on the number of dancers, as many as four couples may be traveling down the center at any one time. When a couple reaches the end of the lines, the partners separate and return to their respective positions, from which they once more begin to move toward the head of the line.

For the spring social dance, the women wear black manta-dresses with white blouses underneath and colorful, lace-trimmed shawls. The men wear kilts, black body paint on their chests, backs, arms, and lower legs, and white body paint around their waists, on their hands, and on their upper legs. All the dancers carry evergreens in their hands, and they sing as they dance without a drummer.

SUN BASKET DANCE. See RAIN DANCE.

SUN DANCE. See RAIN DANCE.

THREE TIMES DANCE. See CLOUD DANCE.

TURTLE DANCE (San Juan). The San Juan turtle dance is one of the few for which the village strictly forbids photography. Although it is performed each year on December 26, it has little to do with Christmas. Instead, it is associated with fertility, youth, agriculture, and rain. The turtle dance is choreographically simple: the dancers, all men, stand in a single line and ântegeh in place with occasional pivots, singing as they dance. New songs are composed each year, and there is no drum accompaniment. The dancers wear kilts but not shirts or leggings, and each ties a turtle-shell rattle to the back of his right knee. Bodies are painted in the same manner as for the spring social dance, and the dancers wear headdresses consisting of a yarn squash blossom and two feathers.

YELLOW CORN DANCE (Nambe). The Nambe Tewas present their version of the yellow corn dance for their patron saint's day celebration on October 4, except every seventh year, when they perform the elk dance. Perhaps because of the October date, this corn dance uses both agricultural and hunting symbols. The women carry ears of corn and evergreens in each hand, and the men carry bows and some arrows in their left hands (see fig. 14). Both men and women wear headbands with three feathers attached at the back. The women dress in black manta-dresses with white shirts underneath and lace-trimmed shawls on top. The men wear white crocheted leggings, kilts, and white shirts. Most of the dance is performed in two parallel lines in which men and women alternate. The dancers are accompanied by a drummer and several male singers.

The San Juan version of this dance is held in late winter or early spring (sometimes at Easter), and the performance begins with a wasa entrance, as described for the butterfly dance. The men do not carry bows and arrows, and the women do not wear the headband with three feathers.

EPILOGUE

Preparing a new edition of this book gave me the opportunity to reflect on the original as an expression of a particular moment in the development of ethnographic research. It also represented a moment in my life and career and a moment in the history of the Tewa communities. I returned to the original text only to find that what I described in the 1970s and 1980s still holds true today. But I also found that in many respects I had obscured or omitted the names and voices of the Tewa people. This new edition gives me the opportunity to bring into sharper focus the perspectives of several Pueblo individuals.

One of the first tasks I set for myself was tracking down the people featured in the original photographs. I knew that this process might be difficult because most of the pictures were taken almost thirty years ago. My search took me to several tribal governors' offices, a casino, a tribal arts and crafts co-op, and several private homes. After returning to New York, I continued the search by using e-mail, letters, and the telephone.

My hope was that by asking many people, I would be able to identify the subjects and then verify these identities by talking to still more. I reasoned that if two or three individuals came up with the same name independently, I could be sure of the identity. What I did not expect was that some people would be reluctant to name a person from another village unless he or she was a relative. For example, Gary Roybal of San Ildefonso was quick to identify a woman from his own village (see fig. 13) and another from Santa Clara (see fig. 17) who was his cousin. But he stated that he would "respectfully defer to Andy Garcia the job of identifying the San Juan dancers." So my next task was to locate Andy. With my

Figure 31. Blue Corn Dance series © *2003 by Mateo Romero, oil on panel, 36 x 50.*

Like a booth at Indian Market in August, the dance can be a time to see old friends and relatives—to pause after a dance set, loosen the belts and bells, wipe off the sweat, and share a bowl of hot red chile....It can be, depending on the dance and the season, physically challenging—a giving of the body with enthusiasm and a friendship of shared experience with other dancers....The dance is made up of intricate patterns, fast steps, deep Pueblo male voices, high notes, and pauses in the staccato drum beats—epiphany.—Mateo Romero

friend and colleague Michael Ennis-McMillan and my niece Marika Stephens, I headed out to San Juan Pueblo in search of him.

It had been years since I had last visited Andy's home, but after a few failed attempts and wrong turns, we found it. Michael went up to inquire whether this was indeed the right house. Andy's wife, Verna, came out to the car and gently took my hand in greeting. Yes, she remembered me, and yes, I could find Andy at the Ohkay Casino. So off to the casino we went, armed with one of my last remaining copies of the first edition, by then out-of-print.

Before my eyes adjusted to the casino's low lighting, I became aware of all the whistles, bells, dropping coins, sirens, and flashing lights designed to announce that some lucky soul had hit a jackpot. At first, I did not spot Andy, even though the place was pretty empty. But following Verna's advice, I had him paged to the winner's circle. As we waited for him, I watched the few Hispanic, Anglo, and Indian patrons, who appeared to be completely mesmerized as they repeatedly pulled the levers or hit the buttons of the machines in front of them.

Andy, who served a term as governor of San Juan Pueblo in 1979, was having lunch in the back with some other current and past tribal officers. Wearing a red baseball cap, he greeted us at the winner's circle with a warm smile. After we reminisced about a 1979 documentary video we had made about his San Juan Youth Dancers, I told him that I was searching for the names of the people featured in the original photographs. He called over his niece, who was working as a uniformed casino security officer, and the two of them carefully studied the images. At first, it seemed that they could easily identify most of them. They commented with pride on how many of the young women were now mothers and, in a couple of cases, already grandmothers. Then my confidence in their answers wavered because Andy admitted that he did not have his glasses with him and some of the images appeared a little fuzzy. Nonetheless, I later followed up with e-mail and found that, with one exception, Andy made the same judgments with his glasses on as he had without them in the casino that day.

Back in the village, we showed the book to several women at O'ke Oweenge, the San Juan tribal arts and crafts cooperative. They began to speculate about the identity of a young dancer, focusing on her manta. This embroidered dress became a central clue for them as they puzzled over her identity. The dress design had its own history, a history that could help them place the dancer in a particular family. At one point, the Anglo husband of one of the women took me aside and muttered, "They probably won't tell you even if they know because it might piss off members of another family." He then added gruffly, "Why couldn't they [meaning me] have gotten the names in the first place?" Of course, I had been asking myself the same question.

On another day, I telephoned Cynthia Dasheno, a Santa Clara woman whose name had come up as possibly that of the person photographed performing in a corn dance at Puye Cliffs (see fig. 17) in 1974. She said that she was at home taking care of a baby but I could come out to show her the photograph. We had a difficult time finding her double-wide mobile home, but after my third call to her on my cell phone, we found our way.

As we parked in front of the house, I realized that the only way in required me to get up five steps to the front door. The wheelchair was out of the question, but I was determined to arrive like anyone else, so with the help of Michael and Marika, I managed to reach the front door. This was to be my first face-to-face encounter with one of the photo subjects, so I wanted to make a good impression. I am sure that I looked pretty strange to Cynthia, who watched the scene from her front window. There I was, with my niece bending over to help me raise each leg so that I could mount another step and Michael hovering close by to make sure that I wasn't going to lose my balance and fall off the side, as the steps had no handrails. The New Mexico sun was high and the day hot by then, making it all the more difficult for me to get up those five steps.

Cynthia graciously welcomed us in, and I showed her the photograph. She said, "It's not me. I didn't think it could be me because while I always participate in the doings by cooking and serving, I haven't actually danced since I was twelve." My spirits sank because the girl in the photograph appeared to be of high-school age. After thanking Cynthia, we got back into the car and left. In a matter of minutes, I was laughing hysterically at my stubbornness, and Marika and Michael joined in. What was I thinking? Why was it so important that I take the book up to her? My only answer is that I had to prove to myself that I could still conduct fieldwork. As it turned out, I later learned that the person in the photograph was one of Cynthia's relatives, Karen Dasheno.

In the end, with help from Andy Garcia, John Garcia, Gary Roybal, and the convenience of e-mail, I was able to confidently identify the following people as the subjects of the 1973 photographs (left to right):

Frontispiece	Dona Tafoya Gutierrez (main dancer)
	Bernice Naranjo (little girl in foreground)
	Norma Suazo Aguilar (woman with coral necklace in background)
	Alfred Naranjo (man in background)
Figure 13	Joyce Da, daughter of Anita and Popovi Da and granddaughter of Maria Poveka Martinez
Figure 17	Karen Dasheno, daughter of Victoria and Teofilo Dasheno
Figure 18	Loretta Trujillo Vigil, daughter of Joe V. and Elizabeth Trujillo

Figure 20   Anthony Garcia, son of Mary Garcia

Figure 26   Male dancers, from left: Tony Trujillo, Steven Trujillo,
               Peter Garcia, Cipriano Garcia
               Female dancers, from left: Julie Martinez,
               Elizabeth Trujillo, Ramona Cruz, Reycita Keevana

Figure 27   Sandra Shije Sandoval

When I spoke to other anthropologists about my project, they were astounded that with all the changes in the Tewa world, such as the presence of new casinos, golf courses, and hotels, individuals still chose to participate in the ritual dance events. Some seriously doubted that I could be correct in my claims of cultural continuity in the dances. They asked skeptically why the Tewas continue to go out to the plaza and dance all day in either the broiling heat of the summer or the bitter cold of winter. I responded that the benefits to the individual and the community must be great enough to motivate participation in spite of the physical and economic costs. In 2002, the price of a single manta might be $50 or more. A child's complete costume cost a minimum of $300, and an adult's outfit up to several thousand dollars.

It seems reasonable to me that the recent economic development has made it more important than ever for the Tewas to dance—to remind themselves of who they are, what values they share, and what makes them stand out from other Americans. But what about the Tewas themselves? How do they explain their continuing participation in village ritual and theatrical performances in the twenty-first century?

According to Andy Garcia, dancing the corn dance or the buffalo dance is necessary community work, "to keep things going." He went on to explain:

> The dances are not done simply for pleasure. They have deep religious meaning. Most honor different creatures such as the buffalo, the dog, deer, antelope, elk, eagle, hawk, and the turtle. Other dances pay respect to corn, clouds, trees—all of nature. Pueblos do not think of themselves as separate from nature or superior to other creatures. Of course, we now go to supermarkets, but we will not forget the ways of our ancestors. If we lose those ways, we lose ourselves.

The critical point is that Tewa people's definitions of themselves as Tewa are intrinsically tied to the ways of their ancestors—the dancers' bodies in motion, the accompanying songs, the costumes, and the paraphernalia. These factors work in concert to define what it is to be Tewa and what it means to be part of a Tewa community.

Gary Roybal of San Ildefonso had this to say about dancing today:

> Why do the people continue to dance as we move into the twenty-first century? This question is easy to answer. We dance because it is our way of life and it is very important for us as Pueblo people to continue the legacy of our forefathers. Without these dances, our Pueblo villages would be silent. We believe the spirit of our ancestors will always be with us, to protect us, to give us strength through our dances.

As a museum technician and Native American liaison for Bandelier National Monument, Gary works with the National Park Service and local pueblos such as San Ildefonso and Cochiti that have ancestral ties to land within the monument.

Nora Naranjo-Morse, a highly regarded artist and resident of Santa Clara Pueblo, offered another response to the question of why the people continue to dance today. She wrote me an e-mail saying,

> As best as I can explain it, Jill, I am transported to the place of sacred ground, where I am suspended. All around me there is motion, color and sound. And I become a part of all that is good. Past sounds echo each time I take a breath, and I am a part of the others who take that breath on the same sacred ground.

In this description, Nora points to the connection between the individual and the collective that is fostered by the dance experience. When she refers to the "echo of past sounds" and the importance of sacred space, she pays homage to the generations that came before her.

When I asked Mateo Romero, another gifted contemporary Pueblo artist, to comment on the question of why people continue to dance, he began by looking back to his father's day. Mateo wrote,

> When my father [Santiago Romero] was still alive, he spoke of how, as a boy at Cochiti Pueblo, the corn dance was an informal affair where only a dozen or so men and women danced. The men simply took off their shirts and put on moccasins, while the women wore sack dresses with cardboard poster–painted tablitas. In some ways, this represents a low point in Pueblo dance. To say the least, times have changed. Now the various dances and the act of dancing in the Rio Grande Pueblo villages have become an intensely stylized, formal, self-conscious act. Dance costumes are highly prized, with an incredible emphasis on lavish craftsmanship. Lines of dancers and one's place in those lines reflect a narcissistic sense of prestige.

This passage is a reminder that participation in the village dances is variable over time. There are low points and high points. The fluctuations may reflect changes in village population, the desire to affirm and display ethnic identity, or improved economic circumstances that make the cost of travel home and acquiring the necessary costumes and paraphernalia more affordable. The period from the early 1970s, when I began my fieldwork, to the early years of the twenty-first century appears to be one of increasingly regular participation.

Mateo went on to consider change further:

> As Pueblo culture moves from pre-modernity to modernity (roughly a century behind the rest of the global post-modern world), Pueblo ideology and values are challenged. But what is lost and what is gained? Perhaps the first noticeable loss is language. Anyone under the age of thirty right now most likely is not fluent in his or her indigenous tongue. Another loss is the esoteric religious societies that are disappearing at an alarming rate. Nevertheless, as language and esoteric religious participation are in decline, dance and art have become the more potent replacement signifiers of culture. Language and society membership still carry tremendous weight in the village, but to the younger post-digital generation these paths to prestige are for the most part unattainable. The youth today are more likely to gravitate to the symbolic power of performance or the celebrity and materialism of contemporary art.

It is not a surprise to me that Native language and membership in religious societies are endangered. With television, radio, and lessons in the public schools being offered only in English, it is no wonder that the younger generation is having difficulty learning the language that is essential for membership in the religious societies.

Finally, Mateo concludes that

> the very core of Pueblo being and harmony is shifting with the speed and pervasiveness of the Internet, satellite TV, MTV, cellular phones, golf courses, tribal casinos, Indian higher education, urban migration and diaspora. But much of what remains is balanced, assimilated, re-made in a new form of Pueblo modernity. Pueblo people have always been in a state of cultural synergy and change. In fact, the essence of Pueblo culture is the dynamic act of balancing and integrating opposites—opposite clans, seasons, peoples, ideas, and cultures.

Both Nora and Mateo are college-educated individuals who participate in the contemporary art scenes of urban centers and enjoy celebrity status within and beyond the Southwest. They show their work in prestigious national venues, such as the National Museum of the American Indian, and university and museum settings. In recent years, each of them was named a Dubin Fellow at the School of American Research. This prestigious fellowship is designed to bring Native artists to work in the studios on the SAR campus. Both Nora and Mateo continue to dance in village events. Mateo even starts some of his paintings with photographs of himself dancing.

A young Tewa man, Mathew J. Martinez, gives us further evidence of the importance of participating in the dances. Martinez wrote the following passage for the 2002 ENIPC visitor guide:

> A central part of my life has been dancing in the pueblo. I believe this is one of the best experiences I've had growing up. Whenever I get asked to dance, I always take the opportunity.... The annual feast day held at each village is a welcoming homecoming occasion for many Pueblo Indians who live and work away from their villages. The constant migration to and from pueblo lands serves as a mediator between the Indian world and mainstream society. It is important that Pueblo people maintain their connection to traditional cultural and religious ceremonies.

In the same publication, Kathy Howkumi of Nambe Pueblo offers her perspective on watching the dances in her village. She reminds us that participation in the dance events takes many forms and the role of the spectator in many respects is just as significant as the roles of dancer, drummer, or singer. She emphasizes the fun, excitement, and beauty and the "special feeling" she gets while watching winter dances.

> There are five times a year that Nambe Pueblo can expect to dance. One of our most important days is our feast day, which is October 4th. The night before feast is vespers, which starts with an evening mass, a procession with bonfires lit throughout the plaza during the procession, and then it's followed by the men dancing in the plaza and the women throwing food and other things to the dancers. It is really a fun and exciting time. It is also pretty in the plaza....[Another time is December 23 and 24.] The night can be cool, but when you're all bundled up and you're watching the dances in the night light, you get that special feeling and blessing, and that's when you know Christmas is here.

Finally, a young man from Santa Clara expressed himself about participating in a dance group that performs in ceremonials and other types of theatrical events away from the village. Darrin Rock wrote for the visitor's guide:

> When I was about three, I started to sing and dance. My uncles and dad

noticed and showed me the correct way to sing. They taught me how to drum, not like it's a toy. My mom says it's understanding the value of the drum and how to use it properly that I know. My great-grandfather, who's from a different pueblo, helps me to understand about respecting my culture. He talks about the significance of the drum and the songs. I've always been watching the elders and ones who drum, and I wanted to be like that. I want to help other people to be more interested and develop knowledge of traditions. One reason we [his ten-member dance troupe] dance every weekend might be that we have business cards, an answering machine that Jeremy [the troupe director] set up, and soon we will have our own website.

This passage points to the process of learning to drum and sing with the help of senior family members, who encourage Darrin to "respect" the traditions. In almost the same breath, however, Darrin acknowledges the importance of business cards, answering machines, and websites. For this young man, the ancient traditions and the modern digital world comfortably coexist.

In the original edition of this book, I included a few quotations about the dances from Pueblo individuals, but I did not identify the speakers. For example, chapter 5, "Keeping the Rituals Alive," ends with the passage, "Our ancestors used to tell us.... Go there to the dance and ask the gods there to give good life—regain your life and make your life a longer life.... You go there like to go to church.... To ask the spirits to give us better life—a longer life—regain life." The speaker of these words was the master song composer Cipriano Garcia. Cip's reputation as a strong singer went beyond his village of San Juan. Tewas from other communities would sit up and listen to his compositions. When Cip passed away, people in the villages knew that it was a great loss.

In the same chapter, I wrote, "As one Tewa man expressed it, 'You've still got to dance with your whole heart because the songs and dance still are sacred and bring beauty, no matter if you dance here or out there.'" These were the words of Andy Garcia, who was explaining to me that the meanings can still be there even when one dances at a theatrical event such as a ceremonial.

In chapter 3, "Theatrical Productions," I wrote about the practice of finishing the dances. I quoted a woman from San Juan saying that practicing for the dances "is not done as often as in the old days—I guess because some of them, they get lazy about it." The woman who spoke these words was Verna Garcia.

Finally, in chapter 2, "Tewa Village Rituals," I wrote,

About the revival efforts, one San Juan man said, "We're trying to get our customs up again instead of them being buried." Another noted, "Within the past few years, more of the younger generation are taking part in it [dance events]—which is good—because we're trying to emphasize to the school kids that this is their doings, their culture, and we want to keep it going." A third San Juan man happily acknowledged the resurgence in dance participation, saying, "The dance lines keep getting longer and younger."

The first speaker quoted in this passage is the song composer Peter Garcia, the second speaker is Andy Garcia, and the third is Tony Garcia.

* * *

This new edition has given me an opportunity to reflect on my years of fieldwork among the Pueblos and to revisit my writings on their dance events. But it was not until the third week of my summer residency at SAR in 2002 that I came to understand more fully what was most important about the work. Perhaps Bruce Grindal and Frank Salamone, editors of an anthology titled *Bridges to Humanity: Narratives on Anthropology and Friendship,* were on the mark when they wrote, "We [anthropologists] must be primarily concerned with human life and experience and continue to affect a voice that allows us to communicate those experiences that, although born of specific cultural circumstances, nonetheless transcend culture and thereby enhance our sensibility and awareness of the human condition" (Grindal and Salamone 1995:viii).

These words took on new meaning for me one morning in Santa Fe when I found myself unable to bend my legs to get out of bed. I called a friend who lives in one of the more conservative pueblos—a pueblo and a friend that long ago I promised never to name in my writings. For years, this friend and I had gone to dances together, and on this particular morning we had planned to go to the Cochiti feast day celebration. But now I told her that I would not be able to meet her there because I had to go to the emergency room at the hospital. She offered to drive to Santa Fe to take me there, but I told her to go on to the dances because my next-door neighbor was going to drive me to the hospital. We said good-bye, and I proceeded to get ready for the hospital. Just as I was about to leave, my friend drove up. She took one look at me and got me into the cab of her fancy new truck. She said that she could not go to Cochiti knowing that I was on my way to the hospital. By that time, I was in too much pain to argue, so off we went to Santa Fe's St. Vincent Hospital.

Once we got to the emergency room, my friend kept me calm and asked questions of the staff for me. She became my hospital advocate and stayed with me all day. We spoke very little, for we both knew that words were unnecessary. Our cultural differences suddenly seemed irrelevant. What really mattered was that two women who had shared many adventures on and off the reservation were now facing together an unfortunate and potentially dangerous turn of events. At that moment, I believe she saw me not as the nosy anthropologist, not as the bumbling tourist, and not as the Anglo whom she mercilessly teased for her ignorance of Pueblo ways and her feeble attempts at speaking the Native language or executing dance steps. Instead, she treated me as the friend who had watched her children grow up and who regularly called from New York just to ask how the family was doing. At that moment, all other aspects of our relationship collapsed, and we became simply two women reaching out to each other with respect, reassurance, and mutual concern. What a profound realization that, after all these years of research and writing, what matters most is this human connection.

Figure 32. Dancing Spirits © *by Nora Naranjo-Morse, monotype print; photograph by Gregory S. Morse.*

REFERENCES

Arnon, Nancy S., and W. W. Hill

1979   Santa Clara Pueblo. In *Handbook of North American Indians,* vol. 9, edited by Alfonso Ortiz. Washington, D.C.: Smithsonian Institution Press.

Bandelier, Adolf F., and Fanny Bandelier

1937   *Historical Documents Relating to New Mexico, Nueva Vizcaya, and Approaches Thereto, to 1773,* vol. 3. Washington, D.C.: Carnegie Institute.

Carroll, Terry Lee

1971   Gallup and Her Ceremonials. Ph.D. diss., University of New Mexico, Albuquerque.

Champe, Flavia Waters

1983   *The Matachines Dance of the Upper Rio Grande.* Lincoln, Neb.: University of Nebraska Press.

Dozier, Edward P.

1961   Rio Grande Pueblos. In *Perspectives in American Indian Culture Change,* edited by Edward H. Spicer. Chicago: University of Chicago Press.

1970   *The Pueblo Indians of North America.* New York: Holt, Rinehart and Winston.

Eickemeyer, Carl, and Lilian Eickemeyer

1895   *Among the Pueblo Indians.* New York: The Merriam Company.

Eliade, Mircea

1954   *Cosmos and History: The Myth of the Eternal Return.* New York: Harper Torchbooks.

Fergusson, Erna

1936   Crusade from Santa Fe. *North American Review* 242: 376–387.

Frost, Richard H.

1980   The Romantic Inflation of the Pueblo Indians. *American West,* 17(I):4–9.

Garcia, Antonio, and Carlos Garcia

1968   Ritual Preludes to Tewa Indian Dances. *Ethnomusicology* 12(2):239–243.

Gilbert, Hope

1940   Reunion at Santa Clara. *New Mexico Magazine* (May):14–15, 42–43.

Grindal, Bruce, and Frank Salamone, eds.

1995   *Bridges to Humanity: Narratives on Anthropology and Friendship.* Long Grove, Ill.: Waveland Press.

Harrington, John P.

1916   The Ethnogeography of the Tewa Indians. In the Bureau of American Ethnology *Annual Report* 29:29–618. Washington, D.C.: U. S. Government Printing Office.

Hartley, Marsden

1920   Red Man Ceremonials. *Art and Archeology* 9(I):7–14.

Huff, J. Wesley

1946   A Quarter Century of Ceremonials. *New Mexico Magazine* (July):13–15, 56–59.

Jackson, H. H.

1882   A Midsummer Fete in the Pueblo of San Juan. *Atlantic Monthly* 49:101–108.

Kurath, Gertrude P., and Antonio Garcia

1970   *Music and Dance of the Tewa Pueblos.* Santa Fe: Museum of New Mexico Press.

Laski, Vera

1959   *Seeking Life.* Memoirs of the American Folklore Society, no. 50.

Leach, Edmund

1976   *Culture and Communication: The Logic by which Symbols Are Connected.* Cambridge: Cambridge University Press.

Lyon, Luther

1979   Los Matachines de Nuevo Mexico. *New Mexico Magazine* (December):72–76.

Ortiz, Alfonso

1965   Dual Organization as an Operational Concept in the Pueblo Southwest. *Ethnology* 4(4):389–396.

1969   *The Tewa World: Space, Time, Being and Becoming in a Pueblo Society.* Chicago: University of Chicago Press.

1972   Ritual Drama and the Pueblo World View. In *New Perspectives on the Pueblos,* edited by Alfonso Ortiz. Albuquerque: University of New Mexico Press.

1977   Some Concerns Central to the Writing of "Indian History." *Indian Historian* 10(1):17–22.

1979a   Oku Shareh: Turtle Dance Songs of San Juan Pueblo. In *New World Records,* no. 301.

1979b   San Juan Pueblo. In *Handbook of North American Indians,* vol. 9, edited by Alfonso Ortiz. Washington, D.C.: Smithsonian Institution Press.

Parsons, Elsie Clews

1929   *Social Organization of the Tewa of New Mexico.* American Anthropological Association Memoir 36.

1939   *Pueblo Indian Religion,* 2 vols. Chicago: University of Chicago Press.

Philip, Kenneth R.

1977   *John Collier's Crusade for Indian Reform, 1920–1954.* Tucson: University of Arizona Press.

Rappaport, Roy A.

1979   *Ecology, Meaning, and Religion.* Richmond, Calif.: North Atlantic Books.

Roediger, Virginia M.

1961   *Ceremonial Costumes of the Pueblo Indians.* Berkeley: University of California Press.

Schechner, Richard

1977   *Essays on Performance Theory, 1970–1976.* New York: Drama Book Specialists.

Sergeant, Elizabeth

1923   Death to a Golden Age. *The New Republic* 35:354–357.

Simmons, Marc

1979   History of the Pueblos since 1821. In *Handbook of North American Indians,* vol. 9, edited by Alfonso Ortiz. Washington, D.C.: Smithsonian Institution Press.

Sloan, John, and Oliver La Farge

n.d.   *Introduction to American Indian Art.* New York: The Exposition of Indian Tribal Arts.

Spicer, Edward H.

1954   Spanish-Indian Acculturation in the Southwest. *American Anthropologist* 56:663–678.

Spinden, Herbert J.

1933   *Songs of the Tewa.* New York: The Exposition of Indian Tribal Arts.

Sweet, Jill D.

1975   Dance of the Rio Grande Pueblo Indians. M.F.A. thesis, University of California, Irvine.

1978   Space, Time, and Festival: An Analysis of a San Juan Event. In *Essays in Dance Research,* edited by Dianne L. Woodruff, *Dance Research Annual 9.* New York: Congress on Research in Dance.

1979   Play, Role Reversal, and Humor: Symbolic Elements of a Tewa Pueblo Navajo Dance. *Dance Research Journal* 12(I):3–12.

1981   Tewa Ceremonial Performances: The Effects of Tourism on an Ancient Pueblo Indian Dance and Music Tradition. Ph.D. diss., University of New Mexico, Albuquerque.

1983   Ritual and Theatre in Tewa Ceremonial Performances. *Ethnomusicology* 27:253–269.

1989   Burlesquing "The Other" in Pueblo Performance. *Annals of Tourism Research* (special edition: Semiotics of Tourism, edited by Dean MacCannell) 16(1):62–75.

1990   The Portals of Tradition: Tourism in the American Southwest. *Cultural Survival Quarterly* 16(2):6–8.

1991   "Let 'Em Loose": Pueblo Indian Management of Tourists. *American Indian Culture and Research Journal* 15(4):59–74.

Sweet, Jill D., and Ruby Bennett

1995   Entering the Field: An Applied Setting in a Postmodern World. Paper presented at the Society for Applied Anthropology meeting, Albuquerque, New Mexico.

Sweet, Jill D., with Ian Berry

2002   *Staging the Indian: The Politics of Representation.* Saratoga Springs, N.Y.: Tang Teaching Museum and Art Gallery.

Thomas, D. H.

1978   *The Southwestern Indian Detour.* Phoenix, Ariz.: Hunter Publishing Company.

Vogt, Evon Z.

1955   A Study of the Southwest Fiesta System as Exemplified by Laguna Fiesta. *American Anthropologist* 57:820–839.

Figure 33. San Ildefonso Pueblo deer danceer with blackened face adn headdress (Photo by Roger Sweet, 1974).

I N D E X